The Modern Book
of
BABIES' NAMES

HILARY SPENCE

LONDON
W. Foulsham & Co. Ltd.
NEW YORK / CAPE TOWN / TORONTO / SYDNEY

W. FOULSHAM & CO LTD
Bennetts Close, Cippenham, Berks. England

*Cover photograph by kind permission
of H. J. Heinz Ltd; Baby Foods.*

© *W. Foulsham & Co. Ltd 1993*
*All rights reserved. Except for use in a review, the reproduction or
utilization of this work in any form or by any electronic, mechanical, or
other means, now known or hereafter invented, including xerography,
photocopying, and recording, and in any information storage and
retrieval system is forbidden without the written permission of the
publisher.*

ISBN 0-572-01174-1

*Printed and bound in Great Britain by
Cox & Wyman Ltd, Reading, Berkshire.*

Choosing a Name

Choosing a name for your new baby should never be taken lightly. Remember, it will be the name by which the child is known to family and friends for the rest of its life. The wrong name can adversely affect your child's life, imparting a stigma which is difficult to come to terms with and which might cause some real unhappiness.

Many parents like to name a child after one or the other grandparents but since fashions in names change almost annually this can have a 'dated' effect. If more than one first name is to be given then the more popular choice should be used first followed by the grandparent's first name. Always check out the resulting initials when first names are written down together with the surname. ANDREW STEPHEN SPENDER may look splendid when written in full but the owner may not be so happy when called upon to merely initial some document or other!

Names tend to have cycles of popularity and for the past forty-six years *The Times* has published an annual list of the most popular names during the preceding year, based on the birth announcements appearing in their columns, and we are grateful for their most recent analysis. While there is little change in the most popular first names for boys – Thomas, James, Alexander and William have remained at the top of the list for a number of years – parents tend to be more adventurous when naming girls, although Charlotte and Sophie have remained very popular in recent years. The numbers in brackets show their position in the previous year's top ten.

MOST POPULAR FIRST NAMES LISTED IN *THE TIMES*

Boys	*Girls*
1. Thomas (1)	1. Charlotte (10)
2. James (2)	2. Sophie (1)
3. Alexander (3)	3. Emily (7)
4. William (4)	4. Olivia (5)
5. Oliver (6)	5. Alice (2)
6. George (7)	6. Eleanor (9)
7. Charles (5)	7. Elizabeth (–)
8. Henry (9)	8. Lucy (4)
9. Edward (8)	9. Hannah (–)
10. Jack (–)	10. Isabella (–)

The Times list tends to include more traditional favourites, rather than names which reflect popular television or other personalties, however, and is also aspirational. Names appearing in the list often become more generally popular a few years later. By comparison, the following is a list of the most popular first names for children born in England and Wales during 1995 and added to the National Health Service Register; it is based on 578,000 babies.

MOST POPULAR FIRST NAMES IN ENGLAND AND WALES

Boys	*Girls*
1. Jack (3)	1. Jessica (3)
2. Daniel (4)	2. Lauren (2)
3. Thomas (1)	3. Rebecca (1)
4. James (2)	4. Sophie (6)
5. Joshua (7)	5. Charlotte (4)
6. Matthew (5)	6. Hannah (5)
7. Ryan (6)	7. Amy (7)
8. Luke (8)	8. Emily (8)
9. Samuel (9)	9. Chloe (11)
10. Jordan (10)	10. Emma (10)

Royal Names

HER MAJESTY THE QUEEN
Elizabeth Alexandra Mary

H.R.H. THE PRINCESS OF WALES
Diana Frances

H.R.H. PRINCESS ANNE
Anne Elizabeth Alice Louise

H.R.H. PRINCESS ANNE'S daughter
Zara Anne Elizabeth

H.M. QUEEN ELIZABETH THE QUEEN MOTHER
Elizabeth Angela Marguerite

H.R.H. PRINCESS MARGARET
Margaret Rose

LADY SARAH ARMSTRONG-JONES
Sarah Frances Elizabeth

H.R.H. PRINCESS BEATRICE OF YORK

H.R.H. PRINCESS EUGINIE OF YORK

H.R.H. THE PRINCE PHILIP, DUKE OF EDINBURGH
Philip

H.R.H. THE PRINCE OF WALES
Charles Philip Arthur George

H.R.H. PRINCE WILLIAM OF WALES
William Arthur Philip Louis

H.R.H. PRINCE ANDREW
Andrew Albert Christian Edward

H.R.H. PRINCE EDWARD
Edward Antony Richard Louis

H.R.H. PRINCESS ANNE'S son
Peter Mark Andrew

VISCOUNT LINLEY
David Albert Charles

H.R.H. PRINCE HENRY OF WALES
Henry Charles Albert David

Girls

Abigail [Hebrew]
' Father rejoiced '. Also the 18th century name for a maidservant.
(Ab, Abbey, Abbie, Abby, Gael, Gail, Gale, Gayl)

Abra [Hebrew]
' Mother of multitudes '.

Acacia [Greek]
The symbol of immortality and resurrection.

Acantha [Greek]
' Thorny '.

Ada [Teutonic]
' Prosperous and joyful '. A popular name in Victorian times.
(Adda, Addie, Addy, Aida, Eda)

Adah [Hebrew]
' The crown's adornment '. One who gives added lustre to the most eminent position.

Adabelle [Combination Ada/Belle]
' Joyous and beautiful '.
(Adabel, Adabela, Adabella)

7

Adalia [Teutonic]
An early Saxon tribal name, the origin of which is not known.

Adamina [Latin]
'From the red earth'. Fem. of Adam.
(Addie, Addy, Mina)

Adar [Hebrew]
'Fire'. Name sometimes given to Jewish daughters born in the sixth month of the Jewish year which is known by the same name.

Adelaide [Teutonic]
'Noble and kind'. A gracious lady of noble birth. A name popular in Britain in the early 19th century, in compliment to Queen Adelaide of Saxe Meiningen, Consort to King William IV.
(Adaline, Adela, Adele, Adelia, Adelina, Adelind, Adeline, Adila, Dela, Della, Edeline, Edelina)

Adelphia [Greek]
'Sisterly'. The eternal friend and sister to mankind.
(Adelfia, Adelpha)

Adina [Hebrew]
'Voluptuous'. One of ripe, mature charm.

Adolpha [Teutonic]
'The noble she-wolf' Fem. of Adolf. The noble matriarch who will sacrifice everything, including life, for her young.
(Adolfa, Adolfina, Adolphina)

Adonia [Greek]
'Beautiful goddess of the resurrection'. The eternal renewal of youth.

Adora [Latin]
'Adored and beloved gift'

Adorna [Latin]
'Adorned with jewels'.

Adorabella [Combination Adora/Bella]
'Beautiful gift'.

Adrienne [Latin]
'Dark lady from the sea'. Fem. of Adrian. A dark, mysterious lady.
(Adria, Adriana, Adriane, Adrianna, Adrianne)

Agatha [Greek]
'Good'. One of impeccable virtue.
(Ag, Agata, Agathe, Agathy, Aggie, Aggy)

Agave [Greek]
'Illustrious and noble'.

Agnes [Greek]
'Pure, chaste, lamblike'. The untouchable virgin.
(Aggie, Agna, Agnella, Annis, Ines, Inez, Nessa, Nessie, Nessi, Nesta, Neysa, Ynes, Ynez)

Aidan [Gaelic]
'Little fire'. A girl with bright red hair.

Aileen [Greek]
A derivative of ' HELEN ', q.v.
(Aleen, Alene, Aline, Eileen, Elene, Ilene, Iline, Illene, Illona, Illeana, Ilona, Isleen)

Aisleen [Gaelic]
' The vision '.

Alana [Celtic]
' Bright, fair one '. A term of
endearment used by the Irish.
*(Alain, Alanna, Alayne,
Alina, Allene, Allyn, Lana,
Lane)*

Alarice [Teutonic]
' Ruler of all '. Fem. of
Alaric.
(Alarica, Alarise)

Alberta [Teutonic]
' Noble and brilliant '. Fem.
of Albert. A nobly born and
highly intelligent girl. Popular
name in Victorian times in
compliment to the Prince
Consort.
*(Albertina, Albertine, Allie,
Berta, Berte, Bertie, Elberta,
Elbertine)*

Albina [Latin]
' White Lady '. One whose
hair and colouring is of the
very fairest.
*(Albinia, Alvina, Aubina,
Aubine)*

Alcina [Greek]
' Strong minded one '. The
legendary Grecian lady who
could produce gold from star-
dust; one who knows her own
mind.

Alda [Teutonic]
' Wise and rich '.
(Eada, Elda)

Aldora [Anglo-Saxon]
' Of noble rank '.
(Aelda, Aeldra)

Aleria [Latin]
' Eagle like '.

Alethea [Greek]
'Truth'
(Alethia)

Alexandra [Greek]
' The helper of mankind '.
Popular name in early 20th
century in compliment to
Queen Alexandra
*(Alex, Alexa, Alexine,
Alexis, Alix, Lexie, Lexine,
Sandy, Sandra, Zandra)*

Alfonsine [Teutonic]
' Noble and ready '. Fem. of
Alphonse.
*(Alphonsina, Alphonsine,
Alonza)*

Alfreda [Teutonic]
' Wise Counsellor '. Fem. of
Alfred. A name popular in
Anglo-Saxon times, but one
which died out after the con-
quest.
*(Alfie, Allie, Elfreda, El-
freida, Elfrieda, Elfrida, Elva,
Elga, Freda)*

Alice [Greek]
' Truth '. A name popularised
in the mid 19th century, when
it was much used by the
Royal Family.
*(Alicia, Alicea, Aletha,
Alethea, Aliss, Alithia, Allys,
Alyce, Alys, Alisa, Alissa,
Allis, Aleece, Alla, Allie,
Ally, Elissa, Elisa)*

Alida [Latin]
' Little winged one '. A girl
who is as small and lithe as
the woodlark.

(*Aleda, Aleta, Alita, Leda, Lita*)

Alima [Arabic]
'Learned in music and dancing'.

Alison [Combination Alice/Louise]
'Truthful warrior maid'.
(*Alie, Allie, Allison, Allson, Lissie, Lisy*)

Alix see **Alexandra**

Allegra [Latin]
'Cheerful'. As blithe as a bird.

Alma [Latin]
'Cherishing spirit'. Name popularly given to girls after the battle of Alma, in the Crimea War.

Almira [Arabic]
(*Elma*)
'Truth without question'.
(*Almeira, Almeria, Elmira*)

Aloha [Hawaiian]
'Greetings'. A romantic name from the Hawaiian Islands.

Alpha [Greek]
'First one'. A suitable name for the first baby, if she is a girl.

Alta [Latin]
'Tall in spirit'.

Althea [Greek]
'The healer'.
(*Aletha, Alethea, Altheta, Althee, Thea*)

Alula [Latin/Arabic]
'Winged one' (Latin). 'The first' (Arabic).
(*Alloula, Allula, Aloula*)

Alura [Anglo-Saxon]
'Divine Counsellor'.

Alva [Latin]
'White lady'.

Alvina [Teutonic]
'Beloved and noble friend'.
(*Alvine, Vina*)

Alyssa [Greek]
'Sane one'. The small white flower Alyssum derives from this name.

Alzena [Arabic]
'The woman'. The embodiment of all feminine charm and virtue.

Amabel [Latin]
'Sweet, lovable one'. A tender, loving, loyal daughter.
(*Amabella, Amabelle*)

Amadea [Latin]
'The beloved of God'.

Amanda [Latin]
'Worthy of being loved'.
(*Manda, Mandie, Mandy*)

Amber [Arabic]
'Jewel'. This name had a surge of popularity in America and Britain in the 1940's, following the publication of the novel *Forever Amber*.

Ambrosine [Greek]
'Divine, immortal one'. Fem. of Ambrose.
(*Ambrosia, Ambrosina*)

Amelia [Teutonic]
'Industrious and striving'.
(Amalia, Amalie, Amealia, Amelea, Ameline, Amelita, Amelie, Emelina, Emeline, Emilia, Emily, Emmeline, Emelie, Mell, Mellie, Mill, Millie)

Amelinda [Spanish]
'Beloved and pretty'.
(Amalinda, Amelinde)

Amena [Celtic]
'Honest'. One of incorruptible truth.
(Amina, Amine)

Amethyst [Greek]
The name of the semi-precious stone which has (it is alleged) the power to ward off intoxication.

Aminta [Greek]
'Protector'. The name of a shepherdess in Greek mythology.
(Amintha, Aminthe)

Amy [French]
'Beloved friend'.
(Aimee, Ami, Amie)

Anastasia [Greek]
'She who will rise again'. The very apt name of the Grand Duchess who was officially killed during the Russian revolution, but who was alleged to be still living until a few years ago.
(Ana, Anstice, Stacey, Stacia, Stacie, Stacy)

Anatola [Greek]
'Woman of the East'. Fem. of Anatole.

(Anatolia, Anatholia)

Andrea [Latin]
'Womanly'. The epitome of feminine charm and beauty.
(Andreana, Aindrea, Andria, Andriana, Andre, Andree)

Anemone [Greek]
'Windflower'. The nymph of Greek mythology who, when pursued by the wind, turned into the flower, anemone.

Angela [Greek]
'Heavenly messenger'. The bringer of good tidings.
(Angelina, Angeline, Angelita, Angel, Angie)

Angelica [Latin]
'Angelic one'. A name often used by Medieval writers to typify the perfect woman.
(Angelique)

Angharad [Welsh]
'Free from shame'

Anita [Hebrew]
'Grace'. A form of Anne, which see.
(Anitra)

Annabelle [Combination Anna/Belle]
(Annabel, Anabel, Annabella, Annie, Annabla, Belle, Bella)

Anne [Hebrew]
'Full of Grace'. One of the most popular feminine names. The name of several British Queens Consort and a Queen Regnant.
(Ann, Anna, Annetta, Annette, Annie, Annora, Anita, Ana, Nan, Nana, Nanna,

Nancy, Nanette, Nanetta, Nanete, Nanine, Nanon, Nina, Ninette, Ninon, Hannah, Hanna)

Annunciata [Latin]
' Bearer of news '. A suitable name for a girl born in March, particularly 24th March, as it derives from the ' Annunciation ' — the announcement of the Virgin's conception.

Anona [Latin]
'Yearly crops'. The Roman Goddess of the Crops.
(Annona, Nonnie, Nona)

Anora [English]
' Light and graceful '.

Anselma [Norse]
' Divinely protected '.
(Anselme, Selma, Zelma)

Anthea [Greek]
' Flowerlike '. One of delicate, fragile beauty.
(Anthia, Bluma, Thea, Thia)

Antonia [Latin]
' Beyond price, excellent '. Fem. of Anthony. A jewel beyond compare.
(Anthonia, Antoinette, Antoni, Antonina, Antoinietta, Antonietta, Toinette, Toni, Netta, Nettie, Netty)

April [Latin]
' The beginning of Spring '. The name of the first month of the Roman calendar and the fourth month of the Julian Calendar.

Ara [Greek]
' Spirit of revenge '. The Grecian Goddess of vengeance and destruction.

Arabella [Latin]
' Beautiful altar '.
(Arabelle, Arabela, Arbelie, Arbelia, Arbel, Bel, Bella, Belle)

Araminta [Greek]
' Beautiful, sweet smelling flower '.

Ardath [Hebrew]
' Field of flowers '.
(Aridatha, Ardatha)

Ardelle [Latin]
' Enthusiasm, warmth '.
(Arda, Ardella, Ardere, Ardis, Ardine, Ardene, Ardeen, Ardella, Ardelis, Ardra)

Areta [Greek]
' Of excellent virtue '. One of untarnished reputation.
(Arete, Aretta, Arette)

Argenta [Latin]
' Silvery one '.
(Argentia, Argente)

Aria [Latin]
' Beautiful melody '.

Ariadne [Greek]
' Holy one '. The mythological maiden who rescued Theseus from his labyrinth.
(Arlana, Ariane, Ariadna)

Ariella [Hebrew]
' God's lioness '.
(Ariel, Ariella, Arielle)

Arlene [Celtic]
' A pledge '.

(Airleas, Arlana, Arleen, Arlen, Arlena, Arlette, Arletta, Arlina, Arline, Arlyne)

Armilla [Latin]
' Bracelet '

Armida [Latin]
' Small warrior '

Armina [Teutonic]
' Warrior maid '.
(Armine, Arminia, Erminie, Erminia)

Arnalda [Teutonic]
' Eagle like ruler '. Fem. of Arnold.

Arva [Latin]
' Pastureland, seashore '.

Arselma [Norse]
' Divine protective helmet '.

Asphodel [Greek]
The wild lily of Greece

Asta [Greek]
' Starlike '.
(Astra)

Astrid [Norse]
' Divine strength '.
(Astra)

Atalanta [Greek]
' Might bearer '. The legendary Greek huntress.
(Atlanta, Atalante)

Atalya [Spanish]
' Guardian '. One who protects heart and home.

Athalia [Hebrew]
' God is exalted '.
(Atalia, Athalea, Athalie, Athie, Attie)

Athena [Greek]
The Greek Goddess.
(Athene, Athenee)

Audrey [Anglo-Saxon]
' Strong and noble '. Derives from the Anglo-Saxon Aethelthryth.
(Audrie, Audry, Audie, Dee)

Augusta [Latin]
' Sacred and majestic '. Popular name in Royal and Noble families in 18th and early 19th century.
(Auguste, Augustina, Augustine, Austine, Gussie, Gusta, Tina)

Aura [Latin]
' Gentle breeze '. A name said to endow its owner with gentility.
(Aure, Aurea, Auria)

Aurelia [Latin]
' Golden '. The girl of the dawn.
(Aura, Aurea, Aurora, Aurelia, Aurelie, Aurel, Aurie, Ora, Oralia, Oralie)

Aurora [Latin]
' Daybreak '.
(Aurore)

Avena [Latin]
' Oatfield '. A girl with rich, golden hair.
(Avene)

Avera [Hebrew]
' Transgressor '.
(Aberah)

Averil [Old English]
  ' Slayer of the Boar '.
  (Avril, Averyl, Avyril)

Avice [French]
  ' Warlike '.
  (Avisa, Hadwisa)

Avis [Latin]
  ' A bird '.
  (Ava, Avi)

Azaliea [Latin]
  ' Dry earth '. From the flower
  of the same name.
  (Azalia, Azalee)

Azura [French]
  ' The blue sky '. One whose
  eyes are ' blue as skies '.

Aaron [Hebrew]
'Exalted'. The brother of Moses.
(Aron, Haroun)

Abbott [Anglo-Saxon]
'Father of the abbey'.
(Abbot, Abott, Abbe)

Abel [Hebrew]
'Breath'. The first recorded murder victim.

Abelard [Teutonic]
'Nobly resolute'.

Abner [Hebrew]
'Father of light'.

Abraham [Hebrew]
'Father of multitudes'. The original patriarch.
(Abram, Abe, Abie, Bram)

Absalom [Hebrew]
'Father of peace'.
(Absolom)

Ace [Latin]
'Unity'.
(Acey)

Ackerley [Anglo-Saxon]
'From the acre meadow'.

Ackley [Anglo-Saxon]
'From the oak tree meadow'.

Adair [Gaelic]
'From the oak tree near the ford'.

Adalard [Teutonic]
'Noble and brave'.
(Adelard, Adhelard)

Adam [Hebrew]
'Of the red earth'. The first man, according to the Bible.

Addison [Anglo-Saxon]
'Adam's son'.

Adelbert See **Albert**

Adin [Hebrew]
'Sensual'.
(Adan)

Adlai [Hebrew]
'My witness, my ornament'.

Adler [Teutonic]
'Eagle'. One of keen perception.

Adney [Anglo-Saxon]
'Dweller on the island'.

Adolph [Teutonic]
'Noble wolf'.
(Adolphe, Adolphus, Adolf, Adolfus, Ad, Dolf, Dolph)

Adon [Hebrew]
'Lord'. The sacred Hebrew word for God.

Adrian [Latin]
'Dark one' or 'Man from the sea'.
(Adrien, Hadrian)

Adriel [Hebrew]
'From God's congregation'.

Aeneas [Greek]
'The much praised one'. The defender of Troy.
(Eneas)

Ahern [Gaelic]
'Horse lord' or 'Horse owner'.
(Aherne, Aherin, Ahearn, Hearne, Hearn)

15

Ahren [Teutonic]
' The Eagle '.

Aidan [Gaelic]
' Little fiery one '.
(Adan, Eden)

Aiken [Anglo-Saxon]
' Little Adam '.
(Aikin, Aickin)

Ainsley [Anglo-Saxon]
' Meadow of the respected
one '.

Alan [Gaelic]
' Cheerful harmony '.
*(Alain, Allan, Allen, Allyn,
Aland, Ailean, Ailin)*

Alaric [Teutonic]
' Ruler of all '.
*(Alarick, Ulric, Ulrich, Ul-
rick, Rich, Richie, Ricy, Rick,
Rickie, Ricky)*

Alastair See **Alexander**

Alban [Latin]
' White complexion '. A man
of outstandingly fair colouring.
(Alben, Albin, Aubin, Alva)

Albern [Anglo-Saxon]
' Noble warrior '.

Albert [Teutonic]
' Noble and illustrious '.
Name which became popular
in Britain after the marriage
of Queen Victoria to Prince
Albert of Saxe-Coborg-Gotha.
*(Aldabert, Adelbert, Delbert,
Elbert, Ailbert)*

Albin See **Alban**

Alcott [Anglo-Saxon]
' Dweller at the old cottage '.

Alden [Anglo-Saxon]
' Old, wise friend '. One on
whom friends could rely.
*(Aldin, Aldwin, Aldwyn,
Elden, Eldin)*

Aldis [Anglo-Saxon]
' From the old house '.
(Aldous, Aldus)

Aldo [Teutonic]
' Old, wise and rich '.

Alder [Anglo-Saxon]
' At the alder-tree '.

Aldrich [Anglo-Saxon]
' Old, wise ruler '.
(Alric, Eldrich, Eldric)

Aldwin See **Alvin**

Aled [Welsh]

Aleron [Latin]
' The eagle '.

Alexander [Greek]
' Helper and protector of
mankind '.
*(Alastair, Allister, Alec, Alex,
Aleck, Alexis, Alick, Alsan-
dair, Alister, Alasdair, Sandie,
Sandy, Sander, Saunders,
Sasha)*

Alfonso See **Alphonse**

Alford [Anglo-Saxon]
' The old ford '.

Alfred [Anglo-Saxon]
' The wise counsel of the elf '.
*(Aelfred, Ailfrid, Alf, Alfie,
Alfy, Al)*

Alger [Teutonic]
'Noble spearman'.
(Algar)

Algernon [French]
'The whiskered one'. The man with a moustache or beard.
(Al, Algie, Algy)

Alison [Anglo-Saxon]
'Son of a nobleman', or 'Alice's son'.
(Allison, Al, Allie)

Allan/Allen See **Alan**

Allard [Anglo-Saxon]
'Noble and brave'.
(Alard, Aethelard, Aethelhard, Athelhard, Ethelard)

Allister See **Alexander**

Almo [Anglo-Saxon]
'Noble and famous'.

Alonzo See **Alphonso**

Aloysius [Latin]
'Famous warrior'.
(Aloys, Lewis, Louis, Ludwig, Alabhaois)

Alphonso [Teutonic]
'Noble and ready'.
(Alfonso, Alphonse, Alfonse, Alphonsus, Alonso, Alonzo)

Alpin [Early Scottish]
'Blond one'. Name borne by the descendants of the earliest Scottish Clan—McAlpin.

Alroy [Gaelic]
'Red haired boy'.

Alston [Anglo-Saxon]
'From the old village'.

Altman [Teutonic]
'Old, wise man'.

Alton [Anglo-Saxon]
'Dweller in the old town'.

Alva See **Alban**

Alvah [Hebrew]
'The exalted one'.
(Alvar)

Alvin [Teutonic]
'Friend of all' or 'Noble friend'.
(Alwin, Alwyn, Alvan)

Amasa [Hebrew]
'Burden bearer'.

Ambert [Teutonic]
'Shining, bright light'.

Ambrose [Latin]
'Belonging to the divine immortals'.
(Ambrosius, Ambroise, Ambros)

Amerigo See **Emery**

Amery See **Amory**

Ammon [Egyptian]
'The hidden'.

Amory [Teutonic]
'Famous ruler'.
(Amery)

Amos [Hebrew]
'A burden'. One used to tackling difficult problems.

Anatole [Greek]
'From the East'.
(Anatol)

Andrew [Greek]
' Strong and manly '. The Patron Saint of Scotland, St. Andrew.
(Andreas, Andre, Aindreas, Anders, Andrien, Andie, Andy)

Aneurin [Celtic]
' Truly golden '.
(Nye)

Angelo [Italian]
' Saintly messenger '.

Angus [Celtic]
' Outstanding and exceptional man '. One of unparalleled strength.

Anscom [Anglo-Saxon]
' Dweller in the secret valley '. An awe-inspiring, solitary man.
(Anscomb)

Annan [Celtic]
' From the stream '.

Ansel [French]
' Nobleman's follower '.
(Ansell)

Anselm [Teutonic]
' Divine helmet '.
(Anse, Ansel, Anselme, Anshelm)

Ansley [Anglo-Saxon]
' From Ann's meadow '.

Anson [Anglo-Saxon]
' Ann's son '.

Anstice [Greek]
' The resurrected '. One who returns to life after death.
(Anstiss)

Anthony [Latin]
' Of inestimable worth '. A man without peer.
(Antony, Antoine, Anton, Anntoin, Antonio, Tony)

Anwell [Celtic]
' Beloved one '.
(Anwyl, Anwyll)

Anyon [Celtic]
' The anvil '. One on whom all the finest characteristics have been forged.

Archard [Tuetonic]
' Sacred and powerful '.
(Archerd)

Archer [Anglo-Saxon]
' The bowman '.

Archibald [Teutonic]
' Noble and truly bold '. A brave and sacred warrior.
(Archimbald, Gilleasbuig, Arch, Archie, Archer, Archy)

Arden [Latin]
' Ardent, fiery, fervent, sincere '. One of intensely loyal nature.
(Ardin)

Ardley [Anglo-Saxon]
' From the domestic meadow '.

Ardolph [Anglo-Saxon]
' The home loving wolf '. The roamer who longs only for home.
(Ardolf)

Argus [Greek]
' The watchful one '. The giant with a hundred eyes, who saw everything at once.

Argyle [Gaelic]
' From the land of the Gaels '.

Aric [Anglo-Saxon]
' Sacred ruler '.
(Rick, Rickie, Ricky)

Aries [Latin]
' A ram '. One born in April,
from the sign of the Zodiac—
Aries.

Arledge [Anglo-Saxon]
' Dweller by the lake where
the rabbit dances '.

Arlen [Gaelic]
' Pledge '.
(Airleas)

Arlie [Anglo-Saxon]
' From the rabbit meadow '.
(Arley, Arly, Harley, Harly)

Armand [Teutonic]
' Man of the army '. The
military man personified.
(Armin, Armond)

Armstrong [Anglo-Saxon]
' Strong arm '. The tough
warrior who could wield a
battle axe.

Arnall [Teutonic]
' Gracious eagle '. The nobleman who is also a gentleman.

Arnett [French]
' Little eagle '.
(Arnatt, Arnott)

Arney [Teutonic]
' The eagle '.
(Arnie, Arne)

Arno [Teutonic]
' Wolf-like eagle '.

Arnold [Teutonic]
' Strong as an eagle '.
*(Arnald, Arnaud, Arne,
Arnie, Arno)*

Artemis [Greek]
' Gift of Artemis '.
(Artemas)

Arthur [Celtic]
' The noble bear man ' or
' Strong as a rock '. The semi-
legendary King of Britain,
who founded the Round
Table.
*(Aurthur, Artair, Artur,
Artus, Art, Artie)*

Arundel [Anglo-Saxon]
' Dweller with eagles '. One
who lives with and shares the
keen sightedness of the eagle.

Arvad [Hebrew]
' The wanderer '.
(Arpad)

Arval [Latin]
' Much lamented '.
(Arvel)

Arvin [Teutonic]
' Friend of the people '. The
first true socialist.

Asa [Hebrew]
' The healer '.

Ascot [Anglo-Saxon]
' Owner of the east cottage '.
(Ascott)

Ashburn [Anglo-Saxon]
' The brook by the ash tree '.

Ashby [Anglo-Saxon]
' Ash tree farm '.

Asher [Hebrew]
'The laughing one'. A happy lad.

Ashford [Anglo-Saxon]
'One who lives in the ford by the ash tree'.

Ashley [Anglo-Saxon]
'Dweller in the ash tree meadow'.
(Lee)

Ashlin [Anglo-Saxon]
'Dweller by the ash tree pool'.

Ashton [Anglo-Saxon]
'Dweller at the ash tree farm'.

Ashur [Semitic]
'The martial one'. One of warlike tendencies.

Aswin [Anglo-Saxon]
'Spear comrade'.
(Aswine)

Atherton [Anglo-Saxon]
'Dweller at the spring farm'.

Atley [Anglo-Saxon]
'One who lives in the meadow'.

Atwater [Anglo-Saxon]
'One who lives by the water'.

Atwood [Anglo-Saxon]
'From the forest'.
(Atwoode, Attwood)

Atwell [Anglo-Saxon]
'From the spring'. One who built his home by a natural well.

Atworth [Anglo-Saxon]
'From the farm'.

Aubert See **Albert**

Aubin [French]
'The blond one'.

Aubrey [Teutonic]
'Elf ruler'. The golden haired king of the spirit world.

Audric [Teutonic]
'Noble ruler'.

Audwin [Teutonic]
'Noble friend'.
(Aldwin, Aldwyn, Adalwine)

August [Latin]
'Exalted one'.
(Augustus, Augustin, Augustine, Austen, Austin, Aguistin, Auguste, Gus, Gussy, Augie)

Avenall [French]
'Dweller in the oat field'.
(Avenel, Avenell)

Averill [Anglo-Saxon]
'Boar like' or 'Born in April'.
(Averil, Averel, Averell, Everild)

Avery [Anglo-Saxon]
'Ruler of the elves'.

Axel [Teutonic]
'Father of peace'.

Axton [Anglo-Saxon]
'Stone of the sword fighter'. The whetstone of the warrior's sword.

Aylmer [Anglo-Saxon]
'Noble and famous'.

Aylward [Anglo-Saxon]
'Awe inspiring guardian'.

Aylworth [Anglo-Saxon]
'Farm belonging to the awe inspiring one'.

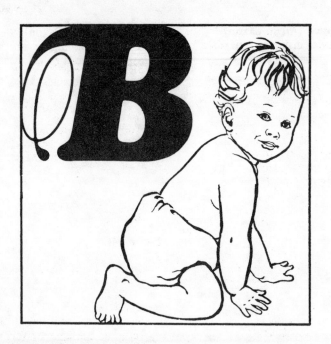

Girls

Bab [Arabic]
'From the gateway'. Also used as dim. of Barbara, *q.v.*

Balbina [Latin]
'She who hesitates'.
(Balbine, Balbinia)

Bambi [Latin]
'The child'. Suitable name for one of tiny stature.
(Orel)

Baptista [Latin]
'Baptized'. A name symbolic of man's freedom from sin through Baptism.
(Baptiste, Batista, Battista)

Barbara [Latin]
'Beautiful stranger'. The lovely, but unknown visitor.
(Bab, Babb, Bas, Barbie, Barbette, Babette, Barbra)

Basilia [Greek]
'Queenly, regal'. Fem. of Basil.

Bathilda [Teutonic]
'Battle commander'. Traditionally one who fought for honour and truth.
(Bathilde, Batilda, Batilde)

Bathsheba [Hebrew]
'Seventh daughter'. Bath-

sheba was the wife of King David in Biblical times.

Beata [Latin]
' Blessed, divine one '. Blessed and beloved of God.
(Bea)

Beatrice [Latin]
' She who brings joy '.
(Beatrix, Beitris, Bea, Bee, Trix, Trixie, Trixy)

Beda [Anglo-Saxon]
' Warrior maiden '.

Belinda [Italian]
' Wise and immortal beauty '.
(Bella, Belle, Linda, Lindie, Lindy)

Bellance [Italian]
' Blonde beauty '.
(Blanca)

Belle [French]
' Beautiful woman '. Can also be used as a dim. of Belinda and Isabelle.
(Bell, Bella, Belva, Belvia)

Bena [Hebrew]
' The wise one '. A woman whose charm is enhanced by wisdom.

Benedicta [Latin]
' Blessed one '. Fem. of Benedict.
(Benedetta, Benedikta, Benita, Benoite, Bennie, Binnie, Dixie)

Benigna [Latin]
' Gentle, kind and gracious '. A great lady.

Berdine [Teutonic]
' Glorious one '.

Berengaria [Teutonic]
' Spearer of bears '. A warrior huntress of renown.

Bernadette [French]
' Brave as a bear '.
(Bernadina, Bernadene, Bernadine, Bernita, Bernardina, Bernie, Berney)

Bernia [Latin]
' Angel in armour '.
(Bernie)

Bernice [Greek]
' Herald of victory '.
(Berenice, Burnice, Berny, Bunny, Veronica)

Bertha [Teutonic]
' Bright and shining '. The Teutonic goddess of fertility.
(Berthe, Berta, Bertie, Berty, Bertina)

Berthilda [Anglo-Saxon]
' Shining warrior maid '.
(Berthilde, Bertilda, Bertilde)

Bertrade [Anglo-Saxon]
' Shining adviser '.
(Bertrada)

Beryl [Greek]
' Precious jewel '. This stone is said to bring good fortune; therefore, the name is also said to give good luck to its user.
(Beryle, Beril, Berri, Berrie, Berry)

Bethel [Hebrew]
' House of God '.
(Beth)

Bethseda [Hebrew]
'House of Mercy'.
(Bethesda)

Beulah [Hebrew]
'The married one'. The traditional wife.
(Beula)

Beverley [Anglo-Saxon]
'Ambitious one'.
(Beverly, Beverlie, Bev, Berry)

Bevin [Gaelic]
'Melodious lady'. One whose voice is so beautiful that even the birds will cease singing to listen to her.
(Bebhinn)

Billie [Teutonic]
'Wise, resolute ruler'. Sometimes used as a diminutive of Wilhelmina.
(Billy, Willa)

Binga [Teutonic]
'From the hollow'.

Binnie See **Sabina**

Birdie [Mod. English]
'Sweet, little bird'.

Blanche [French]
'Fair and white'. A very popular name in medieval times when it was supposed to endow its user with all feminine virtues.
(Blanch, Blanca, Blanka, Blinne, Blinnie. Bluinse, Bianca, Branca)

Blasia [Latin]
'She who stammers'.

Blessin [O. English]
'Consecrated'.
(Blessing)

Bliss [O. English]
'Gladness, joy'.
(Blita, Blitha)

Blodwyn [Welsh]
'White flower'
(Blodwen)

Blossom [O. English]
'Fragrant as a flower'.

Blyth [Anglo-Saxon]
'Joyful and happy'.
(Blith, Blithe, Blythe)

Bonita [Latin]
'Sweet and good'.
(Bona, Bonne, Bonnie, Nita)

Brenda [Teutonic]
'Fiery' or (Irish) 'Raven'.
(Bren)

Brenna [Irish]
'Raven haired beauty'.

Bridget Irish/Celtic]
'Strong and mighty'. Popular name in Ireland, where St. Bridget is Patron Saint.
(Brigid, Brigette, Brigida, Brigitte, Breita, Brieta, Brietta, Brie, Biddie, Biddy, Bridie, Bridey, Brydie)

Briony See **Bryony**

Bronwen [Welsh/Celtic]
'White bosomed'.
(Bronwyn)

Brucie [French]
'From the thicket'. Fem. of Bruce.

Brunella [Italian]
One with brown hair. The
true brunette.
(Brunelle, Bruella, Bruelle)

Brunetta [French]
' Dark haired maiden '.

Brunhilda [Teutonic]
' Warrior heroine '.
(Brunhild, Brunhilde)

Buena [Spanish]
' The good one '.
(Buona)

Bryna [Irish]
' Strength with virtue '. Fem.
of Brian.
(Brina, Briana)

Bryony [Old English]
A twining vine
(Briony)

Bailey [French]
' Steward '. The trusted guardian of other men's properties.
(Baillie, Baily, Bayley)

Bainbridge [Anglo-Saxon]
' Bridge over the white water '.

Baird [Celtic]
' The minstrel '. The ancient bard.
(Bard)

Balbo [Latin]
' The mutterer '.

Baldemar [Teutonic]
' Bold and famous prince '.

Balder [Norse]
' Prince '. The god of Peace.
(Baldur, Baldhere)

Baldric [Teutonic]
' Princely ruler '.
(Baudric)

Baldwin [Teutonic]
' Bold, noble protector '.
(Baudouin, Balduin)

Balfour [Gaelic]
' From the pasture '.

Ballard [Teutonic]
' Strong and bold '.

Bancroft [Anglo-Saxon]
' From the bean field '.

Banning [Gaelic]
' The little golden haired one '.

Barclay [Anglo-Saxon]
' Dweller by the birch tree meadow '.
(Berkeley, Berkley)

Bard See **Baird**

Bardolf [Anglo-Saxon]
' Axe wolf '.
(Bardolph, Bardolphe, Bardulf, Bardulph)

Bardrick [Anglo-Saxon]
' Axe ruler '. One who lived by the battle axe.
(Baldric, Baldrick)

Barlow [Anglo-Saxon]
' One who lives on the barren hills '.

Barnaby [Hebrew]
' Son of consolation '.
(Barnabas, Barney, Barny)

Barnard See **Bernard**

Barnum [Anglo-Saxon]
' Nobleman's house '. Dwelling place of the princely.

Barnett [Anglo-Saxon]
' Noble leader '.
(Barnet)

Baron [Anglo-Saxon]
' Noble warrior '. The lowest rank of the peerage.
(Barron)

Barr [Anglo-Saxon]
' A gateway '.

Barret [Teutonic]
' As mighty as the bear '.
(Barrett)

Barris [Celtic]
' Barry's son '.

Barry [Gaelic]
' Spearlike '. One whose intellect is sharp as a sword.
(Barrie)

Bartholomew [Hebrew]
' Son of the furrows; plough-
man '. One of the twelve
apostles.
*(Bartel, Barthelmey, Barto-
lome, Bartley, Bardo, Barth,
Barthol, Bart, Bat)*

Bartley [Anglo-Saxon]
' Bartholomew's meadow '.

Barton [Anglo-Saxon]
' Barley farmer '.

Bartram [Anglo-Saxon]
' Glorious raven '.
(Barthram)

Baruch [Hebrew]
' Blessed '.
(Barrie, Barry)

Basil [Greek]
' Kingly '. St. Basil the
founder of the Greek Ortho-
dox Church.
*(Basile, Basilio, Basilius,
Vassily)*

Baxter [Teutonic]
' The baker of bread '.
(Bax)

Bayard [Anglo-Saxon]
' Red haired and strong '. The
personification of knightly
courtesy.
(Bay)

Beacher [Anglo-Saxon]
' One who lives by the oak
tree '.
(Beecher, Beach, Beech)

Beagan [Gaelic]
' Little one '.
(Beagen)

Beal [French]
' The handsome '. In the form
' Beau ' used to identify the
smart, well dressed, person-
able men of the 17th and
early 18th cenuturies.
(Beale, Beall, Beau)

Beaman [Anglo-Saxon]
' The bee keeper '.

Beattie [Gaelic]
' Public provider '. One who
supplies food and drink for
the inhabitants of a town.
(Beatie, Beaty, Beatty)

Beau See **Beal**

Beaufort [French]
' Beautiful stronghold '. The
name adopted by the descendants of the union of John of
Gaunt and Katharine Swyn-
ford.

Beaumont [French]
' Beautiful mountain '.

Beck [Anglo-Saxon]
' A brook '.
(Bec)

Beecher See **Beacher**

Belden [Anglo-Saxon]
' Dweller in the beautiful
glen '.
(Beldon)

Bellamy [French]
' Handsome friend '.

Benedict [Latin]
' Blessed '. One blessed by
God.
*(Bendix, Benito, Benoit,
Benot, Bengt, Benedic, Bene-*

dick, Benedix, Bennet, Bennett, Ben, Benny, Dixon)

Benjamin [Hebrew]
' Son of my right hand '. The beloved youngest son.
(Beathan, Ben, Bennie, Benjy, Benny)

Benoni [Hebrew]
' Son of my sorrow '. The former name of the Biblical Benjamin.

Bennett See **Benedict**

Benson [Hebrew]
' Son of Benjamin '.

Bently [Anglo-Saxon]
' From the farm where the grass bends '.
(Bentley)

Benton [Anglo-Saxon]
' From the town on the moors '.

Beresford [Anglo-Saxon]
' From the barley ford '.

Berg [Teutonic]
' The mountain '.

Berger [French]
' The shepherd '.

Berk See **Burke**

Berkeley See **Barclay**

Bernard [Teutonic]
' As brave as a bear '. A courageous warrior.
(Bernhard, Barnard, Barnet, Barnett, Bern, Burnard, Bearnard, Barney, Barny, Bernie, Berny)

Bert See **Albert, Bertram, Egbert, Herbert**

Berthold [Teutonic]
' Brilliant ruler '.
(Bertold, Berthoud, Bert, Bertie)

Berton [Anglo-Saxon]
' Brilliant one's estate '.
(Burton, Burt, Bertie)

Bertram [Anglo-Saxon]
' Bright raven '.
(Bartram, Bertrand)

Bevan [Welsh]
' Son of a noble man '.
(Beaven, Beavan, Beven)

Beverley [Anglo-Saxon]
' From the beaver meadow '.
(Beverly)

Bevis [French]
' Fair view '.
(Beavais)

Bickford [Anglo-Saxon]
' Hewer's ford '.
(Bick)

Bing [Teutonic]
' Kettle shaped hollow '.

Birch [Anglo-Saxon]
' At the birch tree '.
(Birk)

Birkett [Anglo-Saxon]
' Dweller by the birch headland '.
(Birket)

Birley [Anglo-Saxon]
' Cattle shed in the field '.

Birney [Anglo-Saxon]
' Dweller on the brook island '.

Birtle [Anglo-Saxon]
'From the bird hill.

Bishop [Anglo-Saxon]
'The Bishop'.

Black [Anglo-Saxon]
'Of dark complexion'.

Blade [Anglo-Saxon]
'Prosperity, glory'.

Blagden [Anglo-Saxon]
'From the dark valley'.

Blaine [Gaelic]
'Thin, hungry-looking'.
(Blain, Blayn, Blayne)

Blair [Gaelic]
'A place' or 'From the plain'.

Blaise [Latin]
'Stammerer' or 'Firebrand'.
(Blase, Blayze, Blaze)

Blake [Anglo-Saxon]
'Of fair complexion'.

Blakeley [Anglo-Saxon]
'From the black meadow'.

Blakey [Anglo-Saxon]
'Little fair one'.

Bland [Latin]
'Mild and gentle'.

Blane See **Blaine**

Blanford [Anglo-Saxon]
'River crossing belonging to one with grey hair'.
(Blandford)

Blaze See **Blaise**

Bliss [Anglo-Saxon]
'Joyful one'. One who always sees the cheerful side.

Blythe [Anglo-Saxon]
'The merry person'.
(Blyth)

Boaz [Hebrew]
'In the Lord is strength'.
(Boas, Boase)

Boden [French]
'The herald'. The bringer of news.

Bogart [Teutonic]
'Strong bow'.

Bonar [French]
'Good, gentle and kind'.

Boniface [Latin]
'One who does good'.

Boone [Norse]
'The good one'.

Booth [Teutonic]
'From a market'. or 'Dweller in a hut' or 'Herald'.
(Both, Boothe, Boot, Boote)

Borden [Anglo-Saxon]
'From the valley of the boar'.

Borg [Norse]
'Dweller in the castle'.

Boris [Slavic]
'A fighter'. A born warrior.

Boswell [French]
'Forest town'.

Bosworth [Anglo-Saxon]
'At the cattle enclosure'.

Botolf [Anglo-Saxon]
'Herald wolf'.
(Botolph, Botolphe)

Bourke See **Burke**

Bourne [Anglo-Saxon]
' From the brook '.
(Burne)

Bowen [Celtic]
' Descendant of Owen '. A proud Welsh name borne by many descendants of the almost legendary Owen.

Bowie [Gaelic]
' Yellow haired '.

Boyce [French]
' From the woods '. A forester.

Boyd [Gaelic]
' Light haired '. The blond Adonis.

Boyne [Gaelic]
' White cow '. A very rare person.

Bradburn [Anglo-Saxon]
' Broad brook '.

Braden [Anglo-Saxon]
' From the wide valley '.

Bradford [Anglo-Saxon]
' From the broad crossing '.

Bradley [Anglo-Saxon]
' From the broad meadow '.
(Bradly, Brad, Lee)

Brady [Gaelic]
' Spirited one ' or ' From the broad island '.

Brainard [Anglo-Saxon]
' Bold as a raven '. One who knows not fear.
(Brainerd)

Bram See **Abraham**

Bramwell [Anglo-Saxon]
' From the bramble bush spring '.

Bran [Celtic]
' Raven '. The spirit of eternal youth.
(Bram)

Brand [Anglo-Saxon]
' Firebrand '. The grandson of the god, Woden.

Brander [Norse]
' Sword of fire '.

Brandon [Anglo-Saxon]
' From the beacon on the hill '.

Brant [Anglo-Saxon]
' Fiery one ' or ' Proud one '.

Brawley [Anglo-Saxon]
' From the meadow on the hill slope '.

Brendan [Gaelic]
' Little raven ' or ' From the fiery hill '.
(Brendon)

Brent [Anglo-Saxon]
' Steep hill '.

Brett [Celtic]
' Native of Brittany ' or ' From the island of Britain '. One of the original Celts.
(Bret)

Brewster [Anglo-Saxon]
' The brewer '.

Brian [Celtic]
' Powerful strength with virtue and honour '. Brian Boru

the greatest Irish king.
*(Briant, Brien, Bryan, Bryant,
Brion, Bryon)*

Brice [Celtic]
' Quick, ambitious and alert '.
(Bryce)

Bridger [Anglo-Saxon]
' Dweller by the bridge '.

Brigham [Anglo-Saxon]
' One who lives where the
bridge is enclosed '.

Brock [Anglo-Saxon]
' The badger '.
(Broc, Brockie, Brok)

Brockley [Anglo-Saxon]
' From the badger meadow '.

Broderick [Anglo-Saxon]
' From the broad ridge ' or
' Son of Roderick '.
(Broderic)

Brodie [Gaelic]
' A ditch '.
(Brody)

Bromley [Anglo-Saxon]
' Dweller of the broom
meadow '.

Bronson [Anglo-Saxon]
' The brown haired one's
son '.

Brook [Anglo-Saxon]
' One who lives by the
brook '.
(Brooke, Brooks)

Brougher [Anglo-Saxon]
' The fortified residence '.
(Brough)

Broughton [Anglo-Saxon]
' From a fortified town '.

Bruce [French]
' From the thicket '. Robert
the Bruce, Scotland's hero-
king.

Bruno [Teutonic]
' Brown haired man '.

Bryan/Bryant See **Brian**

Bryce See **Brice**

Buck [Anglo-Saxon]
' The buck deer '. A fleet
footed youth.

Buckley [Anglo-Saxon]
' One who dwells by the
buck deer meadow '.

Budd [Anglo-Saxon]
' Herald '. The welcome messenger.

Bundy [Anglo-Saxon]
' Free man '. An enfranchised
serf.

Burbank [Anglo-Saxon]
' Dweller on the castle hill
slope '.

Burch See **Birch**

Burchard [Anglo-Saxon]
' Strong as a castle '.
*(Burckhard, Burkhart, Bur-
gard)*

Burdett [French]
' Little shield '.

Burdon [Anglo-Saxon]
' One who lives by the castle
on the hill '.

Burford [Anglo-Saxon]
' Dweller at the river crossing
by the castle '.

Burgess [Anglo-Saxon]
' Dweller in a fortified town '.
(Bergess, Berger, Berg, Burg)

Burke [French]
' From the stronghold '.
(Berk, Berke, Bourke, Burk, Birke, Birk)

Burkett [French]
' From the little fortress '.

Burl [Anglo-Saxon]
' The cup bearer '. The wine server.

Burley [Anglo-Saxon]
' Dweller in the castle by the meadow '.
(Burleigh)

Burne [Anglo-Saxon]
' A brook '.
(Bourn, Bourne, Burn, Byrne)

Burnaby [Norse]
' Warrior's estate '.

Burnard See **Bernard**

Burnell [French]
' Little one with brown hair '.

Burnett [Anglo-Saxon]
' Little one with brown complexion '.

Burney [Anglo-Saxon]
' Dweller on the island in the brook' .

Burr [Norse]
' Youth '.

Burrell [French]
' One of light brown complexion '.

Burton [Anglo-Saxon]
' Of bright and glorious fame ' or ' Dweller at the fortified town '.
(Berton, Bert, Burt)

Busby [Norse]
' Dweller in the thicket '.

Byford [Anglo-Saxon]
' Dweller by the ford '.

Byram [Anglo-Saxon]
' Dweller at the cattle pen '.
(Byrom)

Byrd [Anglo-Saxon]
' Like a bird '.

Byrle See **Burl**

Byrne See **Bourne**

Byron [French]
' From the cottage ' or ' The bear '.

Girls

Cadence [Latin]
'Rhythmic'. One who is graceful and charming.
(Cadena, Cadenza)

Calandra [Greek]
'Lark'. One who is as light and gay as a bird.
(Calandre, Calandria, Cal, Callie, Cally)

Calantha [Greek]
'Beautiful blossom'. A woman of childlike beauty and innocence.
(Calanthe, Kalantha, Kalanthe, Cal, Cally, Callie)

Caledonia [Latin]
'Scottish lassie'. One who comes from the part of Scotland known in earlier times as Caledonia.
(Caledonie)

Calida [Spanish]
'Ardently loving'. A woman capable of great affection.

Calista [Greek]
'Most beautiful of women'. A name for a girl thought to be beautiful beyond the ordinary.
(Calisto, Kallista, Kallisto)

33

Calla [Greek]
' Beautiful '.

Calliope [Greek]
The muse of poetry

Callula [Latin]
' Little beautiful one '.

Caltha [Latin]
' Yellow flower '.

Calvina [Latin]
' Bald '. Fem. of Calvin. Name sometimes used in strongly Calvinistic families.

Calypso [Greek]
' Concealer '. The legendary sea nymph who held Odysseus captive.
(Kalypso)

Cameo [Italian]
' Sculptured jewel '.

Camilla [Latin]
' Noble and righteous '. The name given to the young and beautiful handmaiden in pagan ceremonies.
(Camille, Camile, Camella, Camelia, Camellia, Cam)

Canace [Latin]
' The daughter of the wind '.
(Kanaka, Kanake)

Candace [Latin]
' Pure, glittering, brilliant white '. One whose purity and virtue is beyond suspicion.
(Candice, Candida, Candie, Candy)

Caprice [Italian]
' Fanciful '.

(Capriccia)

Cara [Celtic or Italian]
' Friend ' (Celtic) or ' Dearest one ' (Italian). A name often used as an endearment for a beloved friend.
(Cariad, Carina, Carine, Kara, Karine, Karina)

Carissa [Latin]
' Most dear one '.
(Caressa, Caresse, Carisse)

Carita [Latin]
' Beloved little one '.

Carma [Sanskrit]
' Destiny '. From the Buddhist ' Karma '—Fate.

Carmel [Hebrew]
' God's fruitful vineyard '.
(Carmela, Carmelita, Carmella, Carma, Carmie, Carmelina, Carmeline, Melina)

Carmen [Latin]
' Songstress '. One who has a beautiful, clear voice.
(Carma, Carmia, Carmina, Carmine, Carmita, Charmaine, Carmacita, Carmencita)

Carnation [French]
' Fresh colour '. One with perfect features and colouring.

Caroline [Teutonic]
' Little woman, born to command '. The power behind the throne; the hand which rocks the cradle and rules the world. One who is all that is feminine, but who rules and controls.

(Carola, Carol, Carole, Carolina, Carline, Charleen, Charlene, Charline, Sharleen, Sharlene, Sharline, Caro, Lina, Line)
This name is the fem. of Charles and can also be used in the form Charlotte.

Cassandra [Greek]
Prophetess ignored by men.
(Cassandre, Cass, Cassie)

Casta [Latin]
' Of pure upbringing '.
(Caste)

Catherine [Greek]
' Pure maiden '. The saint who was martyred on a spiked (Catherine) wheel.
(Catharine, Catharina, Cathleen, Catalina, Caterina, Caitlin, Caitrin, Catriona, Cathy, Cathie, Katharine, Katherine, Katherina, Katharina, Katerine, Kateryn, Kathryn, Katrine, Katrina, Kate, Katy, Kathy, Katie, Kit, Kitty)

Ceara [Irish]
' Spear '. A warrior who wielded her spear to the detriment of her enemies.

Cecilia [Latin]
The Patron saint of Music.
(Cecelia, Cecile, Cecily, Celia, Cecil, Sisile, Sisle, Sileas, Sisley, Sissie, Cele, Ciel, Cissie)

Ceiridwen [Welsh]
The Goddess of Bardism
(Ceri, Kerridwen)

Celandine [Greek]
' Swallow ' or ' yellow water flower '.
(Celandon)

Celene See Selene

Celeste [Latin]
' Heavenly '. A woman of divine beauty.
(Celesta, Celestina, Celestine, Cele)

Celosia [Greek]
' Burning flame '.
(Kelosia)

Cerelia [Latin]
' Spring like '. Woman of spring-blossom beauty.
(Cerealia, Cerellia, Cerelie)

Chandra [Sanskrit]
' The moon who outshines the stars '.
(Candra, Chandre, Candre)

Charity [Latin]
' Benevolent and loving '. One who gives with generosity and affection.
(Charissa, Charita, Charry, Cherry)

Charlotte [Teutonic]
See Caroline.
(Charlotta, Carlotta, Charlie, Carlie, Carla and all the variations of Caroline)

Charmaine [Latin]
' Little song '.
(Carmen, Charmain, Charmian)

Charyl See Charlotte

Cherie [French]
' Dear, beloved one '. A term of endearment.
(Cheri, Cherida, Cherry, Cheryl, Sheryl, Sherry, Sherrie)

Cheryl See **Charlotte** or **Cherie**

Chiquita [Spanish]
' Little one '. A term of endearment for a small girl.

Chloe [Greek]
' Fresh young blossom '. The Greek goddess of unripened grain.
(Cloe, Kloe)

Chlorinda See **Clorinda**

Chriselda See **Crisela**

Christabel [Latin]
' Beautiful bright faced Christian '.
(Christabelle, Christabella, Kristabel, Kristabella, Kristabelle)

Christine [French]
' Christian one '.
(Christina, Christiana, Christiane, Cristina, Cristine, Christian, Chrystal, Crystal, Chris, Chrissie, Chrissy, Crissie, Crissy)

Chryseis [Latin]
' Golden daughter '.

Cilla [French]
' The Cilla flower '.

Cinderella [French]
' Girl of the ashes '. From the fairy tale.
(Cindie, Cindy, Ella)

Clara [Latin]
' Bright, shining girl '. One of clear, outstanding beauty.
(Clare, Claire, Klara, Clareta, Clarette, Clarine)

Clarabella [Latin/French]
' Bright, shining beauty '.
(Clarabelle, Clara, Bella)

Clarinda [Spanish]
' Shining blossom of spring '.
(Claramay)

Claresta [English]
' The most shining one '. A woman to outshine all others.
(Clarista)

Clarice [French]
' Little, shining one '. French form of Clara.
(Clarissa, Clarisse, Clariss, Chloris, Chlaris)

Clarimond [Teutonic]
' Brilliant protector '.
(Clarimonda, Clarimonde, Chlarimonda, Chlarimonde)

Claramae [English]
' Brilliant beauty '.
(Clarinda, Clorinda, Chlarinda, Chlorinda)

Clarissa See **Clarice**

Claudia [Latin]
' The lame one '. Fem. of Claud.
(Claude, Claudette, Claudina, Claudine, Claudie, Gladys)

Clematis [Greek]
' Sweet vine '.

Clemence [Latin]
' Merciful and kind '. One

who tempers justice with mercy.
(Clemency, Clementia, Clementina, Clementine)

Cleopatra [Greek]
'Her father's glory'. A girl who will add lustre to her father's name.
(Cleo)

Cleva [Old English]
'Cliff dweller'. Fem. of Clive.

Cliantha [Greek]
'Flower of glory'.
(Cleantha, Cleanthe, Clianthe)

Clio [Greek]
'She who proclaims'. The Greek Muse of History.

Clorinda [Latin]
'Famed for her beauty'.
(Chlorinda, Chlorinde, Clorinde, Clarinda, Clarinde)

Clotilda [Teutonic]
'Famous battle maiden'. A warrior who fought alongside her father and brothers.
(Clotilde, Clothilda, Clothilde)

Clover [English]
'Meadow blossom'. From the sweet smelling field flower of the same name.
(Clovie)

Clymene [Greek]
'Fame and renown'.

Clytie [Greek]
'Splendid daughter'. The mythical nymph who was turned into a heliotrope, so that she could worship the sun.

Colette [Latin]
'Victorious'. A form of Nicolette.
(Collette, Collete)

Colleen [Gaelic]
'Girl'. The name given to a young girl in Ireland.
(Coleen, Colene, Colline, Coline, Cailin)

Columba [Latin]
'The dove'. One of a peaceful disposition.
(Coline, Columbine, Columbia, Colombe, Colly)

Comfort [French]
'One who gives comfort'. One of the virtue names popular with English and American Puritan families.

Conception [Latin]
'Beginning'.
(Conceptia, Concepcion, Conchita, Concha)

Concordia [Latin]
'Harmony and Peace'.
(Concordina, Concordie, Concordy)

Conradine [Teutonic]
'Bold and wise'. Fem. of Conrad.
(Conradina, Conrada, Connie)

Consolata [Latin]
'One who consoles'.
(Consolation)

Constance [Latin]
'Constant'. One who is firm and unchanging.
(Constantia, Constantina, Constanta, Constanine, Constancy, Constanza, Connie, Con)

Consuela [Spanish]
'Consolation'. The friend when in need.
(Consuelo, Connie)

Cora [Greek]
'The maiden'. From Kore, the daughter of Demeter.
(Corella, Corett, Corette, Corina, Corrina, Corinna, Corinne, Corin, Correna, Coretta, Corrie, Corie)

Corabella [Combination Cora/Bella]
'Beautiful maiden'.
(Corabelle)

Coral [Latin]
'Sincere' or 'From the sea'.
(Corale, Coraline, Coralie)

Cordelia [Welsh]
'Jewel of the sea'. The daughter of Lear, the Sea King.
(Cordelie, Cordie, Delia)

Corissa [Latin/Greek]
'Most modest maiden'.
(Corisse)

Corliss [English]
'Cheerful and kind-hearted'.
(Carliss, Carlissa, Corlissa)

Cornelia [Latin]
'Womanly virtue'.

(Cornela, Cornelle, Cornelie, Cornie, Nela, Nelie, Nelli)

Corona [Spanish]
'Crowned maiden'.
(Coronie)

Cosette [French]
'Victorious army'.
(Cosetta)

Cosina [Greek]
'World harmony'.
(Cosima)

Crescent [French]
'The creative one'.
(Crescentia, Crescenta)

Crispina [Latin]
'Curly haired'. Fem. of Crispin.
(Crispine)

Crystal [Latin]
'Clear'. Also form of Christine.
(Cristal, Chrystal)

Cynara [Greek]
'Artichoke'. A beautiful maiden, protected by thorns.

Cynthia [Greek]
'Moon Goddess'. Another name for Diana, Goddess of the Moon, who was born on Cynthos.
(Cindy, Cyn, Cynth, Cynthie)

Cypris [Greek]
'Born in Cyprus'.
(Cypres, Cipressa, Cypressa)

Cyrena [Greek]
'From Cyrene'. A water nymph, beloved of Apollo.
(Cyrenia, Kyrena, Kyrenia)

Cyrilla [Latin]
  'Lordly one'. Fem. of Cyril.
  (Cirilla, Cirila)

Cytherea [Greek]
  'From Cythera'. Another name for Aphrodite.
  (Cytheria, Cytherere, Cytherine)

Cadby [Norse]
' Warrior's settlement '.

Caddock [Celtic]
' Keenness in battle'. An eager warrior.

Cadell [Celtic]
' Battle spirit '.

Cadman [Celtic]
' Battle man '.

Cadmus [Greek]
' Man from the east'. The legendary scholar who devised the Greek alphabet.

Caesar [Latin]
' Emperor '. From this name, all the meanings of Emperor are derived—Tsar, Kaiser, Shah, etc.
(Cesare, Cesar)

Cain [Hebrew]
' The possessed '. The original murderer.

Calder [Anglo-Saxon]
' The brook '.

Caldwell [Anglo-Saxon]
' The cold spring (or well) '.

Caleb [Hebrew]
' The bold one'. The impetuous hero.
(Cal, Cale)

Caley [Gaelic]
' Thin, slender '.

Calhoun [Gaelic]
' From the forest strip '.

Calvert [Anglo-Saxon]
' Calf minder '.

Calvin [Latin]
' Bald '.
(Calvert, Calvino, Cal)

Camden [Gaelic]
' From the valley which winds '.

Cameron [Celtic]
' Crooked nose '. The founder of the Scottish Clan.
(Cam, Camm)

Campbell [Celtic]
' Crooked mouth '. Founder of Clan Campbell.

Canute [Norse]
' The knot '. Name of the king who tried to hold back the waves.
(Knut, Knute)

Caradoc [Celtic]
' Beloved '.

Carey [Celtic]
' One who lives in a castle '.
(Cary)

Carl See **Charles**

Carleton [Anglo-Saxon]
' Farmers' meeting place '.
(Carlton, Carl)

Carlin [Gaelic]
' Little champion '.
(Carling)

Carlisle [Anglo-Saxon]
' Tower of the castle '.
(Carlile, Carlyle, Carlysle)

Carmichael [Celtic]
' From St. Michael's casle '.

Carney [Gaelic]
' Victorious '. The warrior who never lost a battle.
(Carny)

Carol [Gaelic]
' The champion '. The unbeatable fighter.
(Carroll)

Carollan [Gaelic]
' Little champion '.

Carr [Norse]
' One who dwells beside a marsh '.
(Karr, Kerr)

Carrick [Gaelic]
' The rocky cape '.

Carroll See **Carol**

Carson [Anglo-Saxon]
' Son of the marsh-dweller '.

Carswell [Anglo-Saxon]
' The water cress grower '.

Carter [Anglo-Saxon]
' The cart driver '. One who transports cattle and goods.

Cartland [Celtic]
' The land between the rivers '.

Carvell [French]
' Estate in the marshes '.
(Carvel)

Carvey [Gaelic]
' The athlete '.
(Carvy)

Cary See **Carey**

Casey [Gaelic]
' Brave and watchful '. The warrior who never slept.

Cash See **Cassius**

Casimir [Slavic]
' The proclaimer of peace '.
(Cass, Cassie, Cassy, Kazimir, Kasimir)

Caspar [Persian]
' Master of the treasure '. One trusted to guard the most precious possessions.
(Casper, Gaspar, Gasper)

Cassidy [Gaelic]
' Ingenuity ' or ' curly-haired '.

Castor [Greek]
' The beaver '. An industrious person.

Cathmor [Gaelic]
' Great warrior '.

Cato [Latin]
' The wise one '. One with great worldly knowledge.

Cavan [Gaelic]
' The handsome '. The Irish Adonis!
(Kavan)

Cavell [French]
' Little lively one '. Always up and doing.

Cassius [Latin]
' Vain and conceited '. Never far from a mirror.

Cawley [Norse]
' Ancestral relic '.

Cecil [Latin]
' The unseeing one '.
(Sissil)

Cedric [Celtic]
' Chieftain '.

Chad [Anglo-Saxon]
' Warlike; bellicose '.
(Cadda, Chadda)

Chadwick [Anglo-Saxon]
' Town of the warrior '.

Chalmer [Celtic]
' The chamberlain's son ' or
' King of the household '.
(Chalmers)

Chance [Anglo-Saxon]
' Good fortune '.
(Chaunce, Chauncey)

Chancellor [Anglo-Saxon]
' King's counsellor '. A man
trusted with the highest state
secrets.
*(Chaunceler, Chaunceller,
Chanceller)*

Chandler [French]
' The candle maker '.

Channing [French]
' The canon '.
(Chan, Cannon)

Chapman [Anglo-Saxon]
' The merchant '. The travel-
ling salesmen of medieval
times.

Charles [Teutonic]
' The strong man '. The per-
sonification of all that is
masculine.
*(Carl, Carlos, Carol, Carrol,
Charley, Charlie, Chas, Carlo,
Cary, Carey, Chuck, Karl,
Karol, Tearlach)*

Charlton [Anglo-Saxon]
' Charles's farm '.
(Charleton)

Chase [French]
' The hunter '. One who en-
joys the chase.

Chatham [Anglo-Saxon]
' Land of the soldier '.

Chauncey [French]
' Chancellor; record keeper '.
Also var. of Chance and
Chancellor.
(Chancey, Chaunce)

Cheney [French]
' Oak forest dweller '. A
woodman.
(Cheyney)

Chester [Latin]
' The fortified camp '.
(Cheston, Ches, Chet)

Chetwin [Anglo-Saxon]
' Cottage dweller by the wind-
ing path '.
(Chetwyn)

Cheyney See **Cheney**

Chilton [Anglo-Saxon]
' From the farm by the
spring '.
(Chelton)

Christian [Latin]
' Believer in Christ; a Chris-
tian '.
*(Chris, Christy, Christie,
Kristian, Kristin, Kit)*

Christopher [Greek]
' The Christ carrier '. The
man who carried the infant
Christ across the river.
*(Chris, Christophe, Kit,
Kester, Kris, Kriss, Gille-
cirosd)*

Chuck See **Charles**

Churchill [Anglo-Saxon]
' Dweller by the church on the hill '.

Cian [Gaelic]
' The ancient one '. One who lives long.

Cicero [Latin]
' The chick-pea '.

Clare [Latin]
' Famous one '. (Latin) or ' Bright, illlustrious ' (Anglo-Saxon).
(Clair)

Clarence [Latin/Anglo-Saxon]
' Famous, illustrious one '.
(Clavance)

Clark [French]
' Wise and learned scholar '.
(Clarke)

Claud [Latin]
' The lame '.
(Claude)

Claus See **Nicholas**

Clay [Anglo-Saxon]
' From the clay pit '.

Clayborne [Anglo-Saxon]
' From the brook by the clay pit '.
(Clay, Claiborn, Claybourne)

Clayton [Anglo-Saxon]
' From the clay town ' or ' Mortal man '.

Cleary [Gaelic]
' The scholar '.

Clement [Latin]
' Kind and merciful '.
(Clemence, Clemens, Clem, Clemmy, Clim)

Cleve See **Clive**

Cleveland [Anglo-Saxon]
' From the cliff land '.

Cliff See **Clifford**

Clifford [Anglo-Saxon]
' From the ford by the cliff '.
(Clif, Cliff)

Clifton [Anglo-Saxon]
' From the farm by the cliff '.

Clinton [Anglo-Saxon]
' From the farm on the headland '.
(Clint)

Clive [Anglo-Saxon]
' Cliff '.
(Cleve, Cleeve, Clyve)

Clovis [Teutonic]
An early form of Lewis (Louis)—' Famous warrior '.

Cluny [Gaelic]
' From the meadow '.

Clyde [Celtic]
' Warm ' (Welsh Celtic), ' Heard from the distance ' (Scots Celtic)

Cobb See **Jacob**

Colbert [Anglo-Saxon]
' Brilliant seafarer ' or ' Cool and calm '.
(Colvert, Culbert)

Colby [Norse]
' From the dark country '.

Cole See **Nicholas**

Coleman [Anglo-Saxon/Celtic]
'Follower of Nicholas' (Anglo-Saxon) or 'Keeper of the Doves' (Celtic).
(Colman, Col, Cole)

Colin [Gaelic]
'Strong and virile' or 'The young child' or 'Victorious army'.
(Collin, Colan, Cailean, and all der. of Nicholas)

Collier [Anglo-Saxon]
'Charcoal merchant'.
(Colier, Colis, Collyer, Colyer)

Colter [Anglo-Saxon]
'The colt herder'. A lover of horses.

Colton [Anglo-Saxon]
'From the dark town'.

Colver See Culver

Conan [Celtic]
'High and mighty' or 'Wisely intelligent'.
(Conal, Conant, Connall, Connel, Con, Conn, Kynan, Quinn)

Conlan [Gaelic]
'The hero'.
(Conlin, Conlon)

Conrad [Teutonic]
'Brave counsellor'. One who told what was right; not what the receiver wanted to hear.
(Con, Connie, Cort, Curt, Konrad, Kort, Kurt)

Conroy [Gaelic]
'The wise one'.

Constantine [Latin]
'Firm and unwavering'. Always constant.
(Constantin, Konstantin, Konstantine, Constant, Conn)

Conway [Gaelic]
'Hound of the plain'.

Cooper [Anglo-Saxon]
'Barrel maker'.
(Coop)

Corbett [French]
'The raven'. From the raven device worn by the ancient Vikings.
(Corbet, Corbin, Corbie, Corby)

Corcoran [Gaelic]
'Reddish complexion'.
(Corquoran)

Cordell [French]
'Rope maker'.

Corey [Gaelic]
'Dweller in a ravine'.
(Cory)

Cormick [Gaelic]
'The charioteer'.
(Cormac, Cormack)

Cornelius [Latin]
'Battle horn'.
(Cornell, Cornel, Cornall, Cornal, Neal, Neil)

Cort See Conrad

Corwin [French]
'Friend of the heart'.
(Corwen)

Corydon [Greek]
'The helmeted man'.

Cosmo [Greek]
' The perfect order of the universe '.
(Cosme, Cosimo)

Courtland [Anglo-Saxon]
' One who dwelt on the court land '.
(Court)

Courtenay [French]
' A place '.
(Courtney, Court, Cort, Cortie, Corty)

Covell [Anglo-Saxon]
' Dweller in the cave on the slope '.
(Covill)

Cowan [Gaelic]
' Hollow in the hillside '.

Coyle [Gaelic]
' Battle follower '.
(Coile)

Craddock [Celtic]
' Abundance of love '.
(Caradoc, Caradock)

Craig [Celtic]
' From the stony hill '.

Crandell [Anglo-Saxon]
' Dweller in the valley of the crane '.
(Crandall)

Cranley [Anglo-Saxon]
' From the crane meadow '.

Cranston [Anglo-Saxon]
' From the farmstead where the cranes gather '.

Crawford [Anglo-Saxon]
' From the crow ford '.
(Crowford)

Creighton [Anglo-Saxon]
' From the farm by the creek '.
(Crayton)

Crispin [Latin]
' Curly haired '. St. Crispin, the patron saint of shoemakers.
(Crispen, Crisp, Crepin)

Cromwell [Anglo-Saxon]
' One who lives by a winding spring '. The small rivulet that twists and winds through the countryside.

Crosby [Anglo-Saxon/Norse]
' Dweller at the crossroads ' (Anglo-Saxon) or ' Dweller by the shrine of the cross ' (Norse).
(Crosbey, Crosbie)

Crosley [Anglo-Saxon]
' From the meadow with the cross '.

Culbert See **Colbert**

Cullen [Gaelic]
' Handsome one '.
(Cullan, Cullin)

Culley [Gaelic]
' From the woodland '.
(Cully)

Culver [Anglo-Saxon]
' Gentle as the dove, peaceful'. The symbol of peace.
(Colver)

Curran [Gaelic]
' The resolute hero '. One who would die defending the right.

(Curren, Currey, Currie, Curry)

Curtis [French]
' The courteous one'. A gentleman with perfect manners.
(Curtis, Curt, Kurt)

Cuthbert [Anglo-Saxon]
' Famous and brilliant '. One famed for his high intellect.

Cynric [Anglo-Saxon]
' From the royal line of kings '.

Cyprian [Greek]
' Man from Cyprus '. The birthplace of Venus.
(Ciprian, Cyprien)

Cyrano [Greek]
' From Cyrene '.
(Cyrenaica)

Cyril [Greek]
' The lord '.
(Cyrill, Cyrille)

Cyrus [Persian]
' The sun god '. The founder of the Persian Empire.

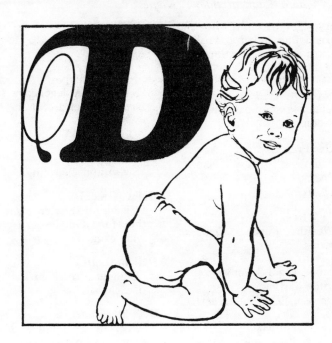

Girls

Dacia [Greek]
'From Dacia'.

Daffodil [Greek]
'Golden flower of spring'.

Dagmar [Norse]
'Glory of the Danes'.

Dahlia
'Of the valley'. From the flower of the same name.

Daisy [Anglo-Saxon]
'The day's eye'. Also a nickname for Margaret (Marguerite), the name of the daisy in French.

Dale [Teutonic]
'From the valley'. An earlier form of Dahlia.

Damita [Spanish]
'Little noble lady'.

Danica [Norse]
'The morning star'.

Danielle [Hebrew]
'God is my judge'. Fem. of Daniel.
(Danielea, Danella, Danelle, Daniela)

Daphne [Greek]
'Bay tree'. Symbol of vic-

47

tory. The nymph who was turned into a laurel bush to escape the attentions of Apollo.

Dara [Hebrew]
' Charity, compassion and wisdom '.

Darcie [French]
' From the fortress '. Fem. of D'Arcy.
(D'Arcie)

Daria [Greek]
' Wealthy queen '. Fem. of Darius.

Darlene [Anglo-Saxon]
' Little darling '.
(Darleen, Darline, Daryl)

Darel [Anglo-Saxon]
' Little dear one '. Another form of Darlene.
(Darelle, Darrelle, Darry, Daryl)

Davina [Hebrew]
' Beloved '. Fem. of David.

Dawn [Anglo-Saxon]
' The break of day '. One who lightens the darkness.

Deanna See **Diana**

Deborah [Hebrew]
' The bee '. An industrious woman who looks only for what is sweet in life.
(Debora, Debra, Debbie, Debby)

Decima [Latin]
' Tenth daughter '.

Dee [Welsh]
' Dark beauty '. Also a dim. of Diana.

Deirdre [Gaelic]
' Sorrow '. A legendary Irish beauty—' Deirdre of the Sorrows '.
(Deidre)

Delcine [Latin]
' Sweet and charming '.

Delia [Greek]
' Visible '. Another name for the Moon Goodess. Also one who came from Delos.

Delicia [Latin]
' Delightful maiden '. ' Spirit of delight '.

Delight [French]
' Pleasure '. One who brings happiness to her family.

Delilah [Hebrew]
' The gentle temptress '. Betrayer of the Biblical Samson.
(Delila, Dalila, Lila)

Della See **Adelaide**

Delma [Spanish]
' Of the Sea '.
(Delmar, Delmare)

Delphine [Greek]
' Calmness and serenity '.
(Delfine)

Delta [Greek]
' Fourth daughter '. The fourth letter of the Greek alphabet.

Demetria [Greek]
' Fertility '. The Goddess of

Fertility.
(Demeter)

Dena [Anglo-Saxon]
' From the valley '.
(Deana, Deane)

Denise [French]
' Wine goddess '. Fem. of
Dionysus, God of wine.
(Denice, Denys)

Desiree [French]
' Desired one '.

Desma [Greek]
' A pledge '.

Desdemona [Greek]
' One born under under an
unlucky star '. After the
heroine of Shakespeare's
Othello.
(Desmona)

Deva [Sanskrit]
' Divine '. The Moon God-
dess.

Devona [English]
' From Devon '. Someone
born in that county, the name
of which means ' People of
the deep valley '.

Dextra [Latin]
' Skilful, adept '.

Diamanta [French]
' Diamond like '. One who is
as precious as the rarest jewel.

Diana [Latin]
' Divine Moon Goddess '.
Roman Goddess of the Moon
and the Chase.
(Deanna, Diane, Dianna,

*Dyana, Dyanna, Dyane, Di,
Dian, Dee)*

Diantha [Greek]
' Divine flower of Zeus '.
(Dianthe, Dianthia)

Dido [Greek]
' Teacher '.

Dinah [Hebrew]
' Judgement '. One whose
understanding is complete.

Dione [Greek]
' The daughter of heaven and
earth '.

Disa [Norse or Greek]
' Lively spirit ' (Norse) or
' Double ' (Greek).

Dixie [French]
' The tenth '.
(Dixey, Dixy, Dixil)

Doanna [Combination
Dorothy/Anna]

Docila [Latin]
' Gentle teacher '.

Dolly See **Dolores** or **Dorothy**

Dolores [Spanish]
' Lady of Sorrow '. Deriving
from ' Our Lady of Sorrows,'
which depicts the seven sad
occasions in the Virgin's life.
*(Delores, Delora, Deloris,
Delorita, Lola, Lolita)*

Domina [Latin]
' The lady '. One of noble
birth.

Dominica [Latin]
' Belonging to the Lord '.
Fem. of Dominic.

(Dominique, Domenica, Dominga)

Donalda [Gaelic]
' Ruler of the world '. Fem. of Donald.

Donata [Latin]
' The gift '.

Donna [Italian]
' Noble lady '.
(Dona)

Dora See **Dorothy**

Dorcas [Greek]
' Graceful '. A girl with the grace of a gazelle.

Dore [French]
' Golden maiden '.

Doreen [Gaelic]
' Golden girl ', alternatively ' The sullen one '.
(Dorene, Dorine, Dori, Dorie, Dory, Dora)

Dorinda [Greek/Spanish]
' Beautiful golden gift '.

Doris [Greek]
' From the sea '. The daughter of Oceanus.
(Doria, Dorice, Dorise, Dorris, Dodi)

Dorothy
' Gift of God '. A form of Theodora.

(Dorothoe, Dora, Doretta. Dorothea, Dorothi, Dorthea, Dorthy, Deel, Dolley, Dollie, Dolly, Dore, Dot, Dotty, Theodora)

Druella [Teutonic]
' Elfin vision '.
(Druilla)

Drusilla [Latin]
' The strong one '. One with patience and fortitude.

Duana [Gaelic]
' Little dark maiden '.
(Duna, Dwana)

Duena [Spanish]
' Chaperon '. A name given to women of good birth who were responsible for the manners and morals of the young girls in their charge.
(Duenna)

Dulcie [Latin]
' Sweet and charming '. One who believes that love is the sweetest thing.
(Dulciana, Dulcibelle, Dulcibella, Delcine, Dulce, Dulcea, Dulcine, Dulcinea)

Durene [Latin]
' The enduring one '.

Dyane See **Diana**

Dacey [Gaelic]
' The southerner '.
(Dacy)

Dag [Norse]
' Day of brightness '.

Dagan [Semitic]
' The earth ' or ' The small fish '.
(Dagon)

Dagwood [Anglo-Saxon]
' Forest of the shining one '.

Dalbert [Anglo-Saxon]
' From the shining valley '.
(Delbert)

Dale [Teutonic]
' Dweller in the valley '.

Dallas [Celtic]
' Skilled ' or ' From the water field '.
(Dal)

Dalton [Anglo-Saxon]
' From the farm in the valley '.

Daly [Gaelic]
' The counsellor '.

Dalziel [Celtic]
' From the little field '.
(Dalziell)

Damon [Greek]
' Tame and domesticated '. The true friend.

Dana [Anglo-Saxon]
' Man from Denmark '.
(Dane)

Danby [Norse]
' From the settlement of the Danish '.

Daniel [Hebrew]
' The Lord is my judge '.
(Daniell, Danielle, Dane, Darnell, Dan, Danny)

Dante See **Durant**

Darby [Gaelic]
'Freeman'. *(Derby)*

Darcy [French]
' From the fortress '.
(Darcie, D'Arcy, Darsey, Darsy)

Darien [Spanish]
A place name

Darius [Greek]
' The wealthy man '.

Darnell [French]
' From the hidden nook '.

Darrell [French]
'Beloved one'. *(Daryl, Darryl)*

Darren [Gaelic]
' Little great one '.

Darton [Anglo-Saxon]
' From the deer forest '.

David [Hebrew]
' The beloved one '. St. David, the patron saint of Wales.
(Dave, Davie, Davy, Davis)

Davin [Scandinavian]
' Brightness of the Finns '.

Davis [Anglo-Saxon]
David's son.

Dean [Anglo-Saxon]
' From the valley '.
(Deane, Dene)

Dearborn [Anglo-Saxon]
' Beloved child ' or ' From the deer brook '.

Dedrick [Teutonic]
' Ruler of the people '.

Deems [Anglo-Saxon]
' The judge's son '.

Delano [French]
' From the nut tree woods '.

Delbert See **Dalbert**

Delling [Norse]
' Very shining one '.

Delmar [Latin]
' From the sea '.
(Delmer)

Delwyn [Anglo-Saxon]
' Bright friend from the valley '.
(Delwin)

Demas [Greek]
' The popular person '.

Demetrius [Greek]
' Belonging to Demeter '.
(Dimitri, Dmitri, Demmy)

Demos [Greek]
' The spokesman of the people '.

Demsey [Gaelic]
' The proud one '.

Dempster [Anglo-Saxon]
' The judge '.

Denby [Norse]
' From the Danish settlement '.

Denley [Anglo-Saxon]
' Dweller in the meadow in the valley '.

Denman [Anglo-Saxon]
' Resident in the valley '.

Dennis [Greek]
' Wine lover '. From Dionysus, the God of Wine.
(Denis, Denys, Dennison, Denzil, Dion, Den, Dennie, Denny, Deny)

Dennison [Anglo-Saxon]
' Son of Dennis '.
(Denison)

Denton [Anglo-Saxon]
' From the farm in the valley '.

Denver [Anglo-Saxon]
' From the edge of the valley '.

Derby See **Darby**

Derek [Teutonic]
' Ruler of the people '.
(Derrick, Derk, Dirk, Derry)

Dermot [Gaelic]
' Free man '.

Derry [Gaelic]
' The red one '.

Derward [Anglo-Saxon]
' Guardian of the deer '.

Derwin [Anglo-Saxon]
' Dearest friend '.

Desmond [Gaelic]
' Man of the world; sophisticated '.

Deverell [Celtic]
' From the river bank '.

Devin [Celtic]
' A poet '.

Devlin [Gaelic]
' Fierce bravery '.

Dewey [Celtic]
' The beloved one '. The
Celtic form of David.

De Witt [Flemish]
' Fair haired one '.

Dexter [Latin]
' The right handed man;
dextrous '.
(Deck, Dex)

Diamond [Anglo-Saxon]
' The shining protector '.

Digby [Norse]
' From the settlement by the
dyke '.

Dillon [Gaelic]
' Faithful '. A true and loyal
man.

Dion See **Dennis**

Dirk See **Derek**

Dixon [Anglo-Saxon]
' Son of Richard ' (Dick's
son).
(Dickson)

Doane [Celtic]
' From the sand dune '.

Dolan [Gaelic]
' Black haired '.

Dominic [Latin]
' Belonging to the Lord; born
on the Lord's day '.
*(Dominic, Domingo, Dominy,
Dom, Nic, Nick, Nickie,
Nicky)*

Donahue [Gaelic]
' Warrior clad in brown '.
(Don, Donn)

Donald [Celtic]
' Ruler of the world '. The
founder of Clan Donald
(MacDonald).
*(Donal, Donnall, Donnell,
Don, Donn, Donnie, Donny)*

Donato [Latin]
' A gift '.

Doran [Celtic]
' The stranger '.

Dorian [Greek]
' Man from Doria '.

Dory [French]
' The golden haired '.

Douglas [Celtic]
' From the dark stream '. One
of the largest Scottish clans.
*(Duglass, Dougal, Dugal,
Dugald, Doug, Douggie,
Douggy, Duggie, Duggy)*

Dow [Gaelic]
' Black haired '.

Doyle [Gaelic]
' The dark haired stranger '.

Drake [Anglo-Saxon]
' The dragon '.

Drew [Celtic]
' The wise one '. Also dim. of
Andrew.

Druce [Celtic]
' Son of Drew '.

Driscoll [Celtic]
' The interpreter '.
(Driscol)

Drury [French]
' The dear one '.

Dryden [Anglo-Saxon]
' From the dry valley '.

Duane See **Dwayne**

Dudley [Anglo-Saxon]
' From the people's meadow '.
*(Dudly, Dud, Duddie,
Duddy)*

Duff [Gaelic]
' Dark complexion '.

Dugal See **Douglas**

Dugan [Gaelic]
' Dark skinned '. The sun-
tanned man.
(Dougan, Doogan)

Duke [French]
' The leader '.

Duncan [Celtic]
' Brown warrior '.
(Dunc)

Dunley [Anglo-Saxon]
' From the meadow on the
hill '.

Dunmore [Celtic]
' From the fortress on the
hill '.

Dunn [Anglo-Saxon]
' Dark skinned '.

Dunstan [Anglo-Saxon]
' From the brown stone hill '.

Durant [Latin]
' Enduring '. One whose
friendship is lasting.
(Durand, Dante)

Durward [Anglo-Saxon]
' The gate keeper '. The
guardian of the drawbridge.

Durwin [Anglo-Saxon]
' Dear friend '.
(Durwyn)

Dwayne [Gaelic/Celtic]
' The small dark man '.
(Gaelic) or ' The singer '
(Celtic).
(Duane)

Dwight [Teutonic]
' The light haired one '.

Dylan [Welsh]
' Man from the sea '.

Girls

Earlene [Anglo-Saxon]
  'Noble woman'. Fem. of Earl.
  (Earlie, Earley, Earline, Erlene, Erline)

Eartha [Old English]
  'Of the earth'.
  (Ertha, Erda, Herta, Hertha)

Easter [Old English]
  'Born at Easter'. The pre-Christian Goddess of Spring.
  (Eastre, Eostre)

Ebba [Anglo-Saxon]

Form of Eve, *q.v.*

Echo [Greek]
  'Repeating sound'. From the Greek nymph who pined away for love.

Eda [Anglo-Saxon]
  'Poetry'.
  (Eada, Edda)

Edana [Gaelic]
  'Little fiery one'. A warmly loving child, whose ardent nature is said to have been bestowed by God himself.
  (Aiden, Aidan, Eidann)

55

Eda [Greek]
' Loving mother of many '.
Also ' Prosperous '.

Eden [Hebrew]
' Enchanting '. The epitome of
all female charm.

Edeline See **Adelaide**

Edina [Scottish]
Another form of Edwina, *q.v.*

Edith [Teutonic]
' Rich gift '.
*(Eadith, Eda, Edythe, Eadie,
Eaidie, Eady, Ede, Edie,
Edithe, Ediva, Editha)*

Edlyn [Anglo-Saxon]
' Noble maiden '.

Edmonda [Anglo-Saxon]
' Rich protector '. Fem. of Ed-
mund.
(Edmunda)

Edna [Hebrew]
' Rejuvenation '. One who
knows the secret of eternal
youth.
(Edny, Ed, Eddie)

Edrea [Anglo-Saxon]
' Powerful and prosperous '.
Fem. of Edric.
(Andrea, Eadrea, Edra)

Edwardina [Anglo-Saxon]
' Rich guardian '. Fem. of
Edward.

Edwina [Anglo-Saxon]
' Rich friend '.
*(Eadwina, Eadwine, Edwine,
Edina, Win, Wina, Winnie)*

Effie [Greek]
' Famous beauty '.
(Effy)

Egberta [Anglo-Saxon]
' Bright, shining sword '. Fem.
of Egbert.
*(Egbertha, Egberthe, Eg-
berte, Egbertina, Egbertine)*

Eglantine [French]
' The wild rose '.
*(Eglantina, Eglintyne, Eglyn-
tine)*

Eileen [Celtic] See **Helen**

Elaine [Greek] See **Aileen**

Elberta See **Alberta**

Eir [Norse]
' Peace and mercy '. The
goddess of healing.

Eirlys [Welsh]
'Snowdrop'

Ekaterina See **Catherine**

Elaine [French] See **Helen**

Elata [Latin]
' Lofty, noble '. A woman of
high birth and beauty.

Eldora [Spanish]
' Gilded one '. From El
Dorado, the land of gold.

Eldrida [Teutonic]
' Old and wise adviser '. Fem.
of Eldred.
(Aeldrida)

Eleanor [French]
A medieval form of Helen.

(Eleanore, Eleanora, Elinor, Elinore, Elinora, Eleonor, Eleonora, Eleonore, Elnore, Leonora, Leonore, Lenora, Lenore, Leanor)

Electra [Greek]
' Brilliant one '.

Elnna See Helen

Elfreda [Teutonic]
' Wise counsellor '. See also Alfreda.
(Elfrida, Elfrieda, Aelfreda)

Elga [Slav]
' Consecrated '.
(Olga)

Elise See Elizabeth

Elizabeth [Hebrew]
' Consecrated to God '. Isabel is another version of this name.
(Elisabeth, Elisa, Elise, Elissa, Eliza, Elyse, Elysa, Elsie, Elsa, Else, Elsbeth, Elspeth, Bess, Bessie, Bessy, Beth, Betsy, Betty, Betta, Bette, Betina, Liza, Lizzy, Lizabeta, Lisbeth, Lizbeth, Libby). And all the various forms of Isabel/Isabella.

Ella [Teutonic]
' Beautiful fairy maiden '. Beauty bestowed by fairies as a birth gift. Also form of Helen.

Ellen See Helen

Ellice [Greek]
' Jehovah is God '. Fem. of Elias.
(Ellis)

Elma [Greek]
' Pleasant and amiable '.

Elmira See Almira

Elna See Helen

Eloise See Louise
' Noble one '. Also form of Elizabeth.

Elsa [Anglo-Saxon]

Elsie/Elspeth See Elizabeth

Elrica [Teutonic]
' Ruler of all '.
(Ulrica)

Elva [Anglo-Saxon]
' Friend of the elves '.
(Elvia, Elvie, Elfie, Elvina)

Elvira [Latin]
' White woman '.
(Albinia, Elvera, Elvire)

Elysia [Latin]
' Blissful sweetness '. From Elysium.

Emerald [French]
' The bright green jewel '.
(Emerant, Emeraude, Esmeralda, Esmeralde)

Emily [Teutonic]
' Industrious '. See Amelia.

Emina [Latin]
' Highly placed maiden '. Daughter of a noble house.

Emma [Teutonic]
' One who heals the universe '. A woman of command.

*(Emmeline, Emelina, Eme-
line, Emelyne, Emmaline,
Ema)*

Emogene See **Imogen**

Ena [Gaelic]
' Little ardent one '. Also dim.
of Eugenia.

Engelberta [Teutonic]
' Bright angel '. One of the
bright defenders of legend.
*(Engelbertha, Engelberthe,
Engelbert)*

Enid [Celtic]
' Purity of the soul '.

Enrica [Italian]
Italian form of Henrietta, *q.v.*

Eolande See **Yolande**

Eranthe [Greek]
' Flower of spring '.

Erda See **Eartha**

Erin [Gaelic]
' From Ireland '. One born in
the Emerald Isle.

Erica [Norse]
' Powerful ruler '. Symbol of
royalty. Fem. of Eric.
(Erika)

Erma [Teutonic]
' Army maid '.
*(Erminia, Ermina, Erminie,
Hermia, Hermine, Hermione)*

Erna [Anglo-Saxon]
' Eagle '. Also variation of
Ernestine.
(Ernaline)

Ernestine [Anglo-Saxon]
' Purposeful one '.
(Erna)

Ertha See **Eartha**

Erwina [Anglo-Saxon]
' Friend from the sea '.

Esmeralda See **Emerald**

Essylt [Welsh]

Esta [Italian]
' From the East '.

Estelle [French]
' Bright star '.
*(Estella, Estrella, Estrelita,
Stella, Stelle)*

Esther [Hebrew]
' The star '.
*(Essa, Etty, Eister, Hester,
Hesther, Hetty, Hessy)*

Ethel [Teutonic]
' Noble maiden '. The
daughter of a princely house.
*(Ethelda, Ethelinda, Etheline,
Ethylyn, Ethyl)*

Ethelinda [Teutonic]
' Noble Serpent '. The symbol
of immortality. Also a var. of
Ethel.

Etta See **Henrietta**

Euclea [Greek]
' Glory '.

Endocia [Greek]
' Of spotless reputation '.
*(Docie, Doxie, Doxy, Eud-
osia, Eudoxia)*

Eudora [Greek]
 ' Generous gift '.
 (Eudore, Dora)

Eugenia [Greek]
 ' Well born '. A woman of a
 noble family.
 *(Eugenie, Genie, Gene, Gina,
 Gena, Ena)*

Eulalia [Greek]
 ' Fair spoken one '.
 (Eulalie, Eula, Lallie)

Eunice [Greek]
 ' Happy and victorious '.

Euphemia [Greek]
 ' Of good reputation '.
 *(Euphemie, Effie, Effy,
 Phemie)*

Eustacia [Latin]
 'Tranquil maiden' 'Fruit-
 ful'.
 *(Eustacie, Stacey, Stacy,
 Stacie)*

Evadne [Greek]

Eve [Hebrew]
 ' Life giver '.
 *(Eva, Eveleen, Evelina, Eve-
 line, Evelyn, Evita, Evonne,
 Evie)*

Evangeline [Greek]
 ' Bearer of glad tidings '.
 *(Evangelina, Eva, Vangie,
 Vancy)*

Evelyn See **Eve**

Eachan [Gaelic]
' Little horse '.
(Eacheann)

Eamonn See **Edmond**

Earl [Anglo-Saxon]
' Nobleman; chief '.
(Erle, Earle, Erl, Errol, Early)

Eaton [Anglo-Saxon]
' From the estate by the river '.

Eben [Hebrew]
' Stone '.

Ebenezer [Hebrew]
' Stone of help '.

Eberhard See **Everard**

Edan [Celtic]
' Flame '.

Edbert [Anglo-Saxon]
' Prosperous; brilliant '.

Edel [Teutonic]
' The noble one '.

Edelmar [Anglo-Saxon]
' Noble and famous '.

Eden [Hebrew]
' Place of delight and pleasure '. The original paradise.

Edgar [Anglo-Saxon]
' Lucky spear warrior '.
(Ed, Eddie, Eddy, Edgard, Ned)

Edmund [Anglo-Saxon]
' Rich guardian '.
(Edmond, Eamon, Eamonn, Ed, Eddie, Eddy, Ned)

Edolf [Anglo-Saxon]
' Prosperous wolf '.

Edric [Anglo-Saxon]
' Fortunate ruler '.

Edsel [Anglo-Saxon]
' A prosperous man's house ' or ' Profound thinker '.

Edson [Anglo-Saxon]
' Edward's son '.
(Edison)

Edwald [Anglo-Saxon]
' Prosperous ruler '.

Edward [Anglo-Saxon]
' Prosperous guardian '.
(Eduard, Ed, Eddie, Eddy, Ned, Neddie, Neddy, Teddy)

Edwin [Anglo-Saxon]
' Prosperous friend '.
(Edlin, Edd, Eddie, Eddy)

Egan [Gaelic]
' Formidable, fiery '.

Egbert [Anglo-Saxon]
' Bright, shining sword '. The name of the first king of all England '.

Ehren [Teutonic]
' Honourable one '.

Einar [Norse]
' Warrior leader '.

Elbert See **Albert**

Elden [Anglo-Saxon]
' Elf Valley '.

Elder [Anglo-Saxon]
' One who lives by an elder tree '.

Eldon [Anglo-Saxon/Teutonic]
' From the holy hill ' (Anglo-
Saxon) or ' Respected elder '
(Teutonic).

Eldridge [Anglo-Saxon]
' Wise adviser '.
(Eldrid, Eldwyn, Eldwin)

Eleazar [Hebrew]
' Helped by God '.
(Elizer, Lazarus, Lazar)

Eli [Hebrew]
' The highest '.
(Ely)

Elias [Hebrew]
' The Lord is God '.
*(Elihu, Elijah, Eliot, Elliott,
Ellis)*

Elijah See **Elias**

Elisha [Hebrew]
' God is my salvation '.

Ellard [Anglo-Saxon]
' Noble, brave '.

Ellery [Teutonic]
' From the elder tree '.
(Elery, Ellerey)

Elliot See **Elias**

Ellis See **Elias**

Ellison [Anglo-Saxon]
' Son of Elias '.

Ellsworth [Anglo-Saxon]
' A farmer; lover of the
land '.

Elmer [Anglo-Saxon]
' Noble; famous '.
(Aylmer)

Elmo [Italian/Greek]
' Protector ' (Italian) or
' Friendly ' (Greek).

Elmore [Anglo-Saxon]
' Dweller by the elm tree on
the moor '.

Elroy [French]
' The king '. The name is sup-
posed to be an anagram of Le
Roi or it may be from the
Spanish El Rey either mean-
ing The King.

Elsdon [Anglo-Saxon]
' Hill belonging to the noble
one '.

Elson See **Ellison**

Elston [Anglo-Saxon]
' Estate of the noble one '.

Elsworth [Anglo-Saxon]
' Estate of the noble one '.

Elton [Anglo-Saxon]
' From the old farm '.

Elvin See **Alwin**

Elvis [Norse]
' All wise '. The prince of wisdom.

Elvy [Anglo-Saxon]
' Elfin warrior '. Though small
in stature he had the heart
of a lion.

Elwell [Anglo-Saxon]
' From the old well '.

Elwin [Anglo-Saxon]
' Friend of the elves '.

Elwood [Anglo-Saxon]
' From an ancient forest '.

Ely See **Eli**

Emery [Teutonic]
'Industrious ruler' or 'Joint ruler'.
(Emmery, Emory, Emerson, Emmerich, Amerigo, Emery)

Emil [Teutonic]
'Industrious'.
(Emile, Emilio, Emlyn)

Emmanuel [Hebrew]
'God is with us'.
(Emanuel, Immanuel, Manuel, Mannie, Manny)

Emmet [Auglo-Saxon]
'The industrious ant'.
(Emmett, Emmit, Emmot, Emmott, Emmy)

Emory See **Emery**

Eneas See **Aeneas**

Ennis [Gaelic]
'The only choice'.

Enoch [Hebrew]
'Consecrated; dedicated; devoted'.

Enos [Hebrew]
'The mortal'.

Ephraim [Hebrew]
'Abounding in fruitfulness'.
(Efrem, Eph)

Erasmus [Greek]
'Worthy of being loved'.
(Erasme, Ras, Rasmus)

Erastus [Greek]
'The beloved'.
(Ras)

Eric [Norse]
'All powerful ruler'.

'Kingly'.
(Erich, Erick, Erik, Rick, Ricky)

Erland [Anglo-Saxon]
'Land of the nobleman'.

Erling [Anglo-Saxon]
'Son of the nobleman'.

Erle See **Earle**

Ermin See **Herman**

Ernest [Anglo-Saxon]
'Sincere and earnest'.
(Ernst, Ernie, Erny)

Errol See **Earl**

Erskine [Celtic]
'From the cliff's height'.

Erwin See **Irwin**

Esmond [Anglo-Saxon]
'Gracious protector'.

Este [Italian]
'Man from the East'.
(Estes)

Ethan [Hebrew]
'Steadfast and firm'.

Ethelbert See **Albert**

Eugene [Greek]
'Nobly born'.
(Gene)

Eustace [Greek]
'Stable, tranquil' or 'Fruitful'.

Evan [Gaelic]
'Well born young warrior'.
Also Welsh form of John.
(Ewan, Ewen, Owen)

Everard [Anglo-Saxon]
' Strong as a boar '.
(Evered, Everett, Eberhard, Eberhart, Ev, Eb)

Everley [Anglo-Saxon]
' Field of the wild boar '.

Ewald [Anglo-Saxon]
' Law powerful '.

Ewert [Anglo-Saxon]
' Ewe herder '. One who tended the ewes in lamb.

Ewing [Anglo-Saxon]
' Friend of the law '.

Ezekiel [Hebrew]
' Strength of God '.
(Zeke)

Ezra [Hebrew]
' The one who helps '.
(Esra, Ez)

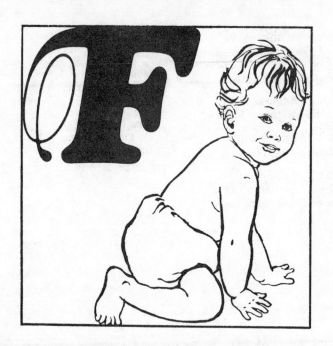

Fabia [Latin]
'Bean grower'.
(Fabiana, Fabianna, Fabienne)

Faith [Teutonic]
'Trust in God'. One who is loyal and true.
(Fae, Fay, Faye)

Fanchon [French]
'Free being'. A derivative of Francoise.

Fanny See Francis

Farica See Frederica

Faustine [Latin]
'Lucky omen'.
(Fausta, Faustina)

Favor [French]
'The helpful one'.
(Favora)

Fawn [French]
'Young deer'. A lithe, swift footed girl.

Fay [French]
'A fairy' or 'A raven' (Irish). A fairy-like person. Also dim. of Faith.
(Fae, Faye, Fayette)

Fayme [French]
' Of high reputation '. Beyond reproach.

Fealty [French]
' Faithful one '. One who is loyal to God, sovereign, country and friend.

Fedora See **Theodora**

Felda [Tuetonic]
' From the field '. For one born at harvest time.

Felicia [Latin]
' Joyous one '. Fem. of Felix.
(Felice, Felicity, Felis, Felicie, Felise, Felicidad)

Fenella [Gaelic]
' White shouldered '.
(Finella)

Feodora See **Theodora**

Fern [Anglo-Saxon]
' Fernlike '.

Fernanda [Teutonic]
' Adventurous '. One who is daring and courageous.
(Ferdinanda, Fernandina)

Fidela [Latin]
' Faithful one '.
(Fidelia, Fidele)

Fifi See **Josephine**

Filipa See **Philippa**

Filma [Anglo-Saxon]
' Misty veil '. An ethereal type of beauty.
(Pholma, Philmen)

Fiona [Gaelic]
' Fair one '.
(Fionn)

Flanna [Gaelic]
' Red haired '.

Flavia [Latin]
' Yellow haired '.

Fleta [Anglo-Saxon]
' The swift one '.

Fleur [French]
' A flower '. French version of Florence.
(Fleurette)

Florence [Latin]
' A flower '.
(Flora, Flore, Floria, Flor, Fiora, Florance, Florinda, Floris, Florine, Firoenza, Florencia, Florentia, Flo, Florrie, Florry, Flossie)

Flower [English]
The English version of Florence.

Fonda [English]
' Affectionate '.

Fortune [Latin]
' Fate '. The woman of destiny.
(Fortuna)

Frances [Latin]
' Free ' or ' Girl from France '.
(Francine, Francyne, Francoise, Francesca, Francisca, Fan, Fanny, Fran, Frannie, Franny, Francy, Frankie)

Freda [Teutonic]
' Peace '. One who is calm and unflurried.
(Frieda, Freida, Frida, Friedie, Freddie)

Frederica [Teutonic]
'Peaceful ruler'.
*(Frederika, Frederique,
Friederik, Fredericka,
Frerike, Frerika, Farica,
Freddie, Freddy)*

Freya [Norse]
'Noble goddess'. The Norse
Goddess of Love—the Norse
equivalent of the Greek
Aphrodite.

Fritzi See **Frederica**

Fronde [Latin]
'Leaf of the fern'.
(Frodis, Frond)

Fulvia [Latin]
'Golden girl'. The daughter
born at high summer.

Fabian [Latin]
'The bean grower' or 'Prosperous farmer'.
(Fabien, Fabe)

Fabron [French]
'The little blacksmith'.
(Fabre, Faber)

Fagan [Gaelic]
'Little, fiery one'.
(Fagin)

Fairfax [Anglo-Saxon]
'Fair haired one'.

Fairley [Anglo-Saxon]
'From the far meadow'.
(Farley, Fairly, Fairlie, Farl)

Falkner [Anglo-Saxon]
'Falcon trainer'. One who trained the birds used in the hunt.
(Faulkner, Faulkener, Fowler)

Fane [Anglo-Saxon]
'Glad, joyful'.

Farand [Teutonic]
'Pleasant and attractive'.
(Farant, Farrand, Ferrand)

Farnell [Anglo-Saxon]
'From the fern slope'.
(Farnall, Fernald, Fernall)

Farnley [Anglo-Saxon]
'From the fern meadow'.
(Fernley)

Farold [Anglo-Saxon]
'Mighty traveller'.

Farr [Anglo-Saxon]
'The traveller'.

Farrell [Celtic]
'The valorous one'.

(Farrel, Ferrell)

Farris See **Ferris**

Faust [Latin]
'Lucky, auspicious'.

Fay [Gaelic]
'The raven'. Symbol of great wisdom.
(Fayette)

Felix [Latin]
'Fortunate'.
(Felice)

Felton [Anglo-Saxon]
'From the town estate'.

Fenton [Anglo-Saxon]
'Dweller of the marshland'.
One who lived by the fens.

Feodor See **Theodore**

Ferdinand [Teutonic]
'Bold, daring adventurer'.
(Fernando, Fernand, Hernando, Ferd, Ferdie, Ferdy)

Fergus [Gaelic]
'The best choice'.
(Fergie)

Fernald See **Farnall**

Ferrand [French]
'One with iron grey hair'.
(Ferant, Ferrant, Ferand)

Ferris [Gaelic]
'The rock'.
(Farris)

Fidel [Latin]
'Advocate of the poor'.
(Fidele, Fidelio)

Fielding [Anglo-Saxon]
'One who lives near the field'.

Filbert [Anglo-Saxon]
(Philbert)
'Very brilliant one'.

Filmer [Anglo-Saxon]
'Very famous one'.
(Filmore, Fillmore)

Findlay See Finlay

Finlay [Gaelic]
'Fair soldier'.
(Finley, Findlay, Findley, Fin, Lee)

Finn [Gaelic]
'Fair haired'.

Firman [Anglo-Saxon]
'Long distance traveller'.
(Farman)

Firmin [French]
'The firm, strong one'.

Fiske [Anglo-Saxon]
'Fish'.

Fitch [Anglo-Saxon]
'The marten'.

Fitz [Anglo-French]
'Son'. Originally in the form of Fils (French for son) the present form was introduced into Britain by the Normans.

Fitzgerald [Anglo-Saxon]
'Son of Gerald'.

Fitzhugh [Anglo-French]
'Son of. Hugh'.

Flann [Gaelic]
'Lad with red hair'.

Flavius [Latin]
'Yellow hatred one'.
(Flavian)

Fleming [Anglo-Saxon]
'The Dutchman'.

Fletcher [French]
'The arrow maker'.

Flinn See Flynn

Flint [Anglo-Saxon]
'A stream'.

Florian [Latin]
'Flowering; blooming'.
(Flory)

Floyd See Lloyd

Flinn [Gaelic]
'Son of the redhaired one'.
(Flinn)

Forbes [Gaelic]
'Man of prosperity; owner of many fields'. The great land-owner.

Ford [Anglo-Saxon]
'The river crossing'.

Forrest [Teutonic]
'Guardian of the forest'.
(Forest, Forester, Forrester, Forster, Foster, Forrie, Foss)

Fortune [French]
'The lucky one'. Child of many blessings.

Foss See Forrest

Fowler See Falkner

Franchot See Francis

Francis [Latin]
'Free man'.
(Frank, Franchot, Franz, Frankie, Fran)

Frank See **Francis** or **Franklin**

Franklin [Anglo-Saxon]
' Free-holder of property '.
He owned his own land to
use as he wished.
*(Frank, Franklyn, Francklin,
Francklyn, Frankie)*

Fraser [French]
' Strawberry ' or ' Curly
haired one '.
(Frazer, Frasier, Frazier)

Frayne [Anglo-Saxon]
' Stranger '.
*(Fraine, Frean, Freen,
Freyne)*

Frederick [Tuetonic]
' Peaceful ruler '. One who
used diplomacy not war.
*(Frederic, Fredric, Fredrick,
Friedrich, Fritz, Frederik,
Fred, Freddie, Freddy)*

Freeman [Anglo-Saxon]
' Born a free man '.

Fremont [Teutonic]
' Free and noble protector '.

Frewin [Anglo-Saxon]
' Free, noble friend '.
(Frewen)

Frey [Anglo-Saxon]
' The lord of peace and pros-
perity '. From the Old Norse
God.

Frick [Anglo-Saxon]
' Bold man '.

Fridolf [Anglo-Saxon]
' Peaceful wolf '.

Fuller [Anglo-Saxon]
' Cloth thickener '.

Fulton [Anglo-Saxon]
' From the field ' or ' Dweller
by the fowl-pen '.

Fyfe [Scottish]
' Man from Fife '.
(Fife, Fyffe)

Girls

Gabrielle [Hebrew]
'Woman of God'. The bringer of good news.
(Gabriel, Gabriella, Gabriele, Gabriela, Gaby, Gabbie)

Gaea [Greek]
'The earth'. The Goddess of the Earth.
(Gaia)

Gail/Gale See **Abigail**

Galiena [Teutonic]
'Lofty maiden'. A tall girl of lofty mien.
(Galiana)

Garda See **Gerda**

Gardenia [Latin]
'White, fragrant flower'.

Garland [French]
'Crown of blossoms'.

Garnet [English]
'Deep red haired beauty'.
(Garnette)

Gay [French]
'Lively'.
(Gai)

Gayle See **Abigail**

Gazella [Latin]
'The antelope'. One who is graceful and modest.

Gelasia [Greek]
'Laughing water'. One who is like a fresh and gurgling stream.
(Gelasie)

Gemma [Latin]
'Precious stone'.
(Gemmel)

Gena/Gina See **Eugenia, Regina**

Geneva [French]
'Juniper tree'. Also var. of Genevieve.
(Genvra, Genevre)

Genevieve [French]
'Pure white wave'.
(Genevra, Genevre)

Georgina [Greek]
'Girl from the farm'. Fem. of George.
(Georgiana, Georgana, Georgia, Georgene, Georgette, Georgine, Girogia, Georgy, Georgie)

Geraldine [Teutonic]
'Noble spear carrier'.
(Geraldina, Gerhardine, Geralda, Gerry, Giralda, Jeraldine, Jeroldine, Jerri, Jerry)

Geranium [Greek]
'Bright red flower'.

Gerda [Norse]
'Protected one'. One who has been strictly brought up and protected.

Germaine [French]
'From Germany'.
(Germain)

Gertrude [Teutonic]
'Spear maiden'. One of the Valkyrie.
(Gertruda, Gertrud, Gertrudis, Gert, Gertie, Gerty, Trudie, Trudy, Gartred)

Ghislaine [French]

Giacinta See **Hyacinth**

Gilberta [Teutonic]
'Bright pledge'. Fem. of Gilbert.
(Gilberte, Gilbertha, Gilberthe, Gilbertina, Gilbertine, Gillie, Gilly)

Gilda [Celtic]
'God's servant'.

Gillian [Latin]
'Young nestling'. Also der. of Juliana.
(Jillian, Jill, Jillie, Gill, Gillie)

Ginerva See **Guinevere** or **Geneva**

Ginger See **Virgina**

Giselle [Teutonic]
'A promise'. One who stands as a pledge for her family.
(Gisella, Gisela, Gisele)

Gitana [Spanish]
'The gipsy'.

Githa See **Gytha**

Gladys [Celtic]
' Frail delicate flower '. Celtic version of Claudia (the lame).
(Gladine, Gladis, Gladdie, Glad, Gwyladys, Gwladys, Gleda)

Gleda [Anglo-Saxon]
Old English version of Gladys.

Glenna [Celtic]
' From the valley '. One of the oldest names on record.
(Glenda, Glynis, Glenn)

Gloria [Latin]
' Glorious one '. An illustrious person. This name was often used of Queen Elizabeth I by her sycophantic courtiers.
(Gloire, Glori, Glory, Gloriana, Glorianna, Gloriane, Glorianne)

Glynis See **Glenna**

Godiva [Anglo-Saxon]
' Gift of God '.
(Godgifu)

Goldie [Anglo-Saxon]
' Pure gold '.
(Golda)

Grace [Latin]
' The graceful one '.
(Gracia, Grazia, Gracie, Grayce, Girosal, Engracia)

Greer [Greek]
' The watchful mother '. The eternal matriarch.
(Gregoria)

Greta See **Margaret**

Griselda [Teutonic]
' Grey heroine '.
(Griselde, Grishelda, Grishelde, Grishilda, Grishilde, Grizelda, Selda, Zelda)

Guda [Anglo-Saxon]
' The good one '.
(Goda)

Guenna see **Guinevere** or **Gwendoline**

Guida [Latin]
' The guide '.

Guilla See **Wilhelmina**

Guinevere [Celtic]
' White phantom '.
(Guinivere, Guenevere, Gwenhwyvar, Jennifer)

Gunhilda [Norse]
' Warrior maid '.
(Gunhilde)

Gustava [Scandinavian]
' Staff of the Goths '.
(Gustave, Gussie, Gussy)

Gwendoline [Celtic]
' White browed maid '.
(Gwendolen, Gwendolene, Gwendolyn, Gwendolyne, Gwenda, Gwennie, Gwen, Gwyn, Wendy)

Gwyneth [Welsh]
'Blessed'

Gypsy [Anglo-Saxon]
' The wanderer '. See also Gitana.
(Gipsy)

Gytha [Anglo-Saxon]
' The war like '.
(Githa)

Gabriel [Hebrew]
' Messenger of God '. The archangel who announced the birth of Christ.
(Gabe, Gabbie, Gabie, Gabby)

Gable [French]
' The small Gabriel '.

Gage [French]
' A pledge '. The glove that was given as an earnest of good faith.

Gale [Celtic]
' The lively one '.
(Gail)

Galen [Gaelic]
' Little bright one ' or (Greek) ' The helper '.

Gallagher [Gaelic]
' Eager helper from oversea '.

Galloway [Celtic]
' Man from the stranger gaels '.
(Galway, Gallway)

Galton [Anglo-Saxon]
' Lease holder of an estate '.

Galvin [Gaelic]
' Bright, shining white ' or ' The sparrow '.
(Galvan, Galven)

Gamaliel [Hebrew]
' The recompense of the Lord '.

Gannon [Gaelic]
' Little blond one '.

Gardiner [Teutonic]
' A gardener; a flower lover '.
(Gardner, Gardener)

Garey See **Gary**

Garfield [Anglo-Saxon]
' War or battle field '.

Garland [Anglo-Saxon]
' From the land of the spears '.

Garman [Anglo-Saxon]
' The spearman '.

Garmond [Anglo-Saxon]
' Spear protector '.
(Garmon, Garmund)

Garner [Teutonic]
' Army guard; noble defender '.

Garnet [Latin]
' A red seed; pomegranate seed '.

Garnett [Anglo-Saxon]
' Compulsive spear man '. He struck first and challenged afterwards.

Garnock [Celtic]
' One who dwells by the river alder '.

Garrett [Anglo-Saxon]
' Mighty spear warrior '.
(Garett, Garret, Garritt, Gerard, Garrard)

Garrick [Anglo-Saxon]
' Spear ruler '.

Garroway [Anglo-Saxon]
' Spear warrior '.
(Garraway)

Garth [Norse]
'From the garden'.

Garton [Anglo-Saxon]
'The dweller by the triangular shaped farm'.

Garvey [Gaelic]
'Rough peace'. Peace obtained after victory!
(Garvie)

Garvin [Teutonic]
'Spear friend'.
(Garwin)

Garwood [Anglo-Saxon]
'From the fir trees'.

Gary [Anglo-Saxon]
'Spearman'.
(Gari, Garey, Garry)

Gaspar [Persian]
'Master of the treasure'. One of the Magi.
(Caspar, Casper, Gasper, Kaspar, Kasper, Jasper)

Gaston [French]
'Man from Gascony'.

Gawain [Celtic]
'The battle hawk'.
(Gawaine, Gavin, Gavan, Gaven, Gawen)

Gayle See **Gale**

Gaylord [French]
'The happy noble man'.
(Gayler, Galor, Gallard)

Gaynor [Gaelic]
'Son of the blond haired one'.

Geary [Anglo-Saxon]
'The changeable'.

(Gearey, Gery)

Gene See **Eugene**

Geoffrey [Teutonic]
'God's Divine peace'.
(Godfrey, Jeffery, Jeffrey, Jeffry, Jeffers, Jeff, Geof, Geoff)

George [Greek]
'The farmer'. The Patron Saint of England.
(Georges, Georgie, Geordie, Gordie, Gordy, Georgy, Georg, Jorge, Jorin, Joris, Jurgen)

Gerald [Teutonic]
'Mighty spear ruler'.
(Geraud, Giraud, Gearalt, Garold, Gereld, Gerrald, Jereld, Jerold, Jerald, Jerrold, Gerry, Gery, Jerry, Ger, Jer)

Gerard [Anglo-Saxon]
'Spear strong; spear brave'.
(Gerrard, Gerhard, Gerhardt, Gearard, Gerry)

Gervase [Teutonic]
'Spear vassal'.
(Gervais, Jarvis, Jervis, Jarvey, Jarv, Ger)

Gibson [Ango-Saxon]
'Son of Gilbert'.

Gideon [Hebrew]
'Brave indomitable spirit' or 'The destroyer'.

Gifford [Teutonic]
'The gift'.
(Giffard, Gifferd)

Gilbert [Anglo-Saxon]
'Bright pledge; a hostage'.

(Gil, Gill, Gillie, Gib, Gibb, Bert, Gilibeirt, Gilleabart)

Gilby [Norse]
'The pledge; a hostage'.
(Gilbey)

Gilchrist [Gaelic]
'The servant of Christ'.
(Gilecriosd)

Giles [Latin/French]
'Shield bearer' (Latin) or 'Youthful shaveling' (French).
(Gilles, Gil)

Gillet [French]
'Little Gilbert'.

Gilmer [Anglo-Saxon]
'Famous hostage'. An eminent knight taken captive in battle.

Gilmore [Gaelic]
'St. Mary's servant'.
(Gillmore, Gilmour)

Gilroy [Latin/Gaelic]
'The king's servant' (Latin) or 'The red haired one's servant' (Gaelic).

Girvin [Gaelic]
'Little rough one'.
(Girvan, Girven)

Gladwin [Anglo-Saxon]
'Kind friend'.

Glanville [French]
'Dweller on the oak tree estate'.
(Glanvil)

Glen [Celtic]
'From the valley'.
(Glenn, Glyn, Glynn)

Godfrey See **Geoffrey**

Glendon [Celtic]
'From the fortress in the Glen'.

Glyn See **Glenn**

Goddard [Teutonic]
'Divinely firm'. Firm in the belief and trust in God.
(Godard, Godart, Goddart)

Godfrey See **Geoffrey**

Goodwin [Anglo-Saxon]
'Good friend; God's friend'.
(Godwin, Godwine, Godewyn)

Golding [Anglo-Saxon]
'Son of the golden one'.

Goldwin [Anglo-Saxon]
'Golden friend'.

Gordon [Anglo-Saxon]
'From the cornered hill'.
(Gordan, Gorden, Gordie, Gordy)

Gorman [Gaelic]
'Small, blue eyed lad'.

Gouveneur [French]
'The Governor; the ruler'.

Gower [Celtic]
'The pure one'.

Grady [Gaelic]
'Illustrious and noble'.

Graham [Teutonic]
'From the grey lands'. One

from the country beyond the mists.
(Graeme)

Granger [Anglo-Saxon]
' The farmer '.

Grant [French]
' The great one '.

Grantland [Anglo-Saxon]
' From the great lands '.

Granville [French]
' Dweller in the big town '.
(Grandville, Granvil, Grandvil)

Grayson [Anglo-Saxon]
' The bailiff's son '.

Greeley [Anglo-Saxon]
' From the grey meadow '.

Gregory [Greek]
' The watchful one '. Someone ever vigilant.
(Greg, Gregor, Gregg, Greiogair, Greagoir)

Gresham [Anglo-Saxon]
' From the grazing meadow '.

Griffith [Celtic]
' Fierce, red haired warrior '.
(Griffin, Gruffydd, Rufus)

Griswold [Teutonic]
' From the grey forest '.

Grover [Anglo-Saxon]
' One who comes from the grove '.

Gunther [Teutonic]
' Bold warrior '.
(Gunnar, Gunner, Gunter, Gunar, Guntar, Gunthar)

Gustave [Scandinavian]
' Staff of the Goths '.
(Gustav, Gustaf, Gustavus, Gus)

Guthrie [Celtic]
' War serpent; war hero ' or ' From the windy country '.
(Guthry)

Guy [French/Teutonic/Latin]
' The guide ' (French); ' The warrior ' (Teutonic); ' Life ' (Latin).
(Guido, Guyon, Wiatt, Wyatt)

Gwynn [Celtic]
' The blond one '.
(Gwyn, Guin)

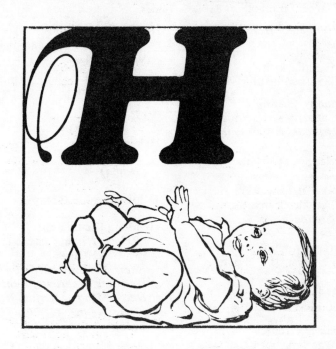

Girls

Hadria See **Adrienne**

Hadwisa See **Avice**

Hagar [Hebrew]
' Forsaken '.

Haidee [Greek]
' Modest, honoured '. A maid renowned for her natural modesty.

Halcyone [Greek]
' The king fisher '. The mythological Greek who was turned into a bird when she drowned herself.
(Halcyon)

Haldana [Norse]
' Half Danish '.

Halfrida [Teutonic]
' Peaceful heroine '. A diplomat not a warrior.
(Halfreida, Halfrieda, Hallie, Frida, Freida, Frieda)

Halimeda [Greek]
' Sea thoughts '. One who is drawn to the sea.
(Hallie, Meda)

Hannah See **Anne**

Haralda [Norse]
' Army ruler '. Fem. of Harold.

*(Haraldina, Harolda, Harold-
ina)*

Harika [Turkish]
'Most beautiful'

Harmony [Latin]
' Concord and harmony '.
(Harmonia, Harmonie)

Harriet See **Henrietta**

Hazel [English]
' The hazel tree '.
(Aveline)

Heather [Anglo-Saxon]
' Flower of the moors '.

Hebe [Greek]
Goddess of Youth

Hedda [Teutonic]
' War '. A born fighter.

Helen [Greek]
'Light'.
According to tradition, the
most beautiful woman,
Helen of Troy. There are so
many variations of this
name, that it is not possible
to list them all. A representa-
tive selection:
*(Helena, Helene, Eleanor,
Eleanore, Elinor, Elenor,
Elinore, Elinora, Elenore,
Elenora, Elaine, Elane, Ella,
Ellen, Ellyn, Ellene, Elena,
Ileane, Ilena, Ilona, Illona,
Illone, Aileen, Aisleen, Eileen,
Isleen, Leonora, Leonore,
Lenora, Leora, Lora, Lana,
Leona, Nora, Norah, Nell,
Lena, Lina)*

Helga [Teutonic]
' Pious, religious and holy '.
Var. of Olga.

Helice [Greek]
' Spiral '.
(Helixa)

Helma [Teutonic]
' A helmet '.
(Hilma)

Heloise See **Louise**

Henrietta [Teutonic]
' Ruler of home and estate '.
Fem. of Henry.
*(Harriet, Harriette, Harriot,
Harriotte, Henriette, Henrika,
Hattie, Hatty, Hettie, Hetty,
Etta, Netta, Netie, Yetta,
Eiric)*

Hera [Latin]
' Queen of the heaven '. The
wife of the ruler of the
Heaven, Zeus.

Herleva See **Arlene**

Hermia See **Hermione**

Hermione [Greek]
' Of the earth '. The daughter
of Helen of Troy '.
*(Hermia, Hermina, Hermine,
Herminia)*

Hermosa [Spanish]
' Beautiful '.

Hertha See **Eartha**

Hesper [Greek]
' The evening star '.
(Hespera, Hesperia)

Hester See **Esther**

Hiberna [Latin]
'Girl from Ireland'.
(Hibernia)

Hibiscus [Latin]
'The marshmallow plant'.

Hilary [Latin]
'Cheerful one'. One who is always happy.
(Hilaria, Hilaire)

Hilda [Teutonic]
'Battle maid'. A handmaiden of the warriers of Valhalla.
(Heidi, Hilde, Hildie, Hild, Hildy)

Hildegarde [Teutonic]
'Battle stronghold'.

Hildemar [Teutonic]
'Battle celebrated'.

Hildreth [Teutonic]
'Battle adviser'.
(Hildretha)

Hilma See **Helma**

Holda [Novse]
'Muffled'
(Holde, Holle, Hulda)

Holly [Anglo-Saxon]
'Bringer of good luck'. The child born during the Christmas season.
(Hollie)

Honey [English]
'Sweet one'. A term of endearment, especially in the U.S.

Honora [Latin]
'Honour'.
(Honor, Honour, Honoria, Honey, Noreen, Norine, Nora, Norah, Norrey, Norrie, Norry)

Hope [Anglo-Saxon]
'Cheerful optimism'. Another 'virtue' name.

Horatia [Latin]
'Keeper of the hours'. Fem. of Horace.
(Haracia, Horacia)

Hortense [Latin]
'Of the garden'. One with green fingers.
(Hortensia)

Huberta [Teutonic]
'Brilliant mind'. One with intelligence above the ordinary.
(Hubertha, Huberthe)

Huette [Anglo-Saxon]
'Brilliant thinker'. Fem. of Hugh.
(Hugette, Hugette, Huetta,

Hulda See **Holda**

Hyacinth [Greek]
'Hyacinth flower'.
(Hyacintha, Hyacinthia, Jacintha, Jacinthia, Cynthie, Cynthis, Jackie)

Hypatia Greek]
'Highest'.

Hackett [Teutonic]
'The small woodsman'. The apprentice forester.
(Hacket)

Hadden [Anglo-Saxon]
'From the heath valley'.
(Haddan, Haddon)

Hadley [Anglo-Saxon]
'From the heath meadow'.

Hadwin [Anglo-Saxon]
'Battle companion'.

Hagen [Gaelic]
'The young one'.
(Hagan, Haggan, Haggen)

Hagley [Anglo-Saxon]
'From the hedged meadow'.

Haig [Anglo-Saxon]
'One who lives in an enclosure'. Popular name for boys during early part of 20th century, in compliment to the Field Marshal Lord Haig.

Hakon [Norse]
'From an exalted race'.
(Haakon, Hako)

Hal See **Harold, Henry**

Halbert [Anglo-Saxon]
'Brilliant hero'.

Halden [Norse]
'Half Danish'.
(Haldan, Halfdan, Haldane)

Hale [Anglo-Saxon]
'From the hall'.

Haley [Gaelic]
'The ingenious one'. One with a scientific intelligence.

Halford [Anglo-Saxon]
'From the ford by the manor house'.

Hall [Anglo-Saxon]
'Dweller at the manor house'.

Hallam [Anglo-Saxon]
'One who lives on the hill slopes'.

Halley [Anglo-Saxon]
'From the Manor House meadow' or 'Holy'.

Halliwell [Anglo-Saxon]
'The dweller by the holy well'.

Hallward [Anglo-Saxon]
'Guardian of the Manor House'.
(Halward)

Halsey [Anglo-Saxon]
'From Hal's island'.
(Halsy)

Halstead [Anglo-Saxon]
'From the manor house place'.
(Halsted)

Halton [Anglo-Saxon]
'From the estate on the hill slope'.

Hamal [Arabic]
'The lamb'. A very gentle person.

Hamar [Norse]
'Symbol of ingenuity'. A great gift for invention.
(Hammar)

Hamilton [Anglo-Saxon/
French]
'Sheep enclosure' (A.S) or
'From the mountain village
(F).

Hamish See **James**

Hamlet [Teutonic]
' Little village '.

Hamlin [Teutonic]
' Small home lover '.
*(Hamelin, Hamlyn, Hame-
lyn)*

Hanford [Anglo-Saxon]
' From the high ford '.

Hannibal
The hero of Carthage

Hank See **Henry**

Hanley [Anglo-Saxon]
' From the high meadow '.
(Handley, Henleigh, Henley)

Hans See **John**

Hansel [Scandinavian]
' Gift from the Lord '.

Harbert See **Herbert**

Harbin See **Herbert**

Harcourt [French]
' From a fortified court '.

Harden [Anglo-Saxon]
' From the valley of the
hare '.

Harding [Anglo-Saxon]
' Son of the hero '.

Hardwin [Anglo-Saxon]
' Brave friend '.
(Harwin, Hardwyn, Harwyn)

Hardy [Teutonic]
' Bold and daring '.
(Hardey, Hardie, Hardi)

Harford [Anglo-Saxon]
' From the hare ford '.
*(Herford, Hereford, Hare-
ford)*

Hargrove [Anglo-Saxon]
' From the hare grove '.
*(Hargrave, Hargreave, Har-
greaves)*

Harlon [Teutonic]
' From the battle land '.
(Harland)

Harley [Anglo-Saxon]
' From the hare meadow '.
*(Arley, Harden, Harleigh,
Hartley, Hartleigh, Arlie,
Harl, Hart)*

Harlow [Anglo-Saxon]
' The fortified hill '. An army
camp on the hillside.

Harman/Harmon See **Herman**

Harold [Anglo-Saxon]
' Army commander '. A
mighty general.
*(Harald, Herold, Hereld,
Herrick, Harailt, Hal, Harry)*

Harper [Anglo-Saxon]
' The harp player '. The wan-
dering minstrel.

Harris [Anglo-Saxon]
' Harold's son '.
(Harrison)

Harry See **Harold, Henry**

Hart [Anglo-Saxon]
' The hart deer '.

81

Hartford [Anglo-Saxon]
'The river crossing of the deer'.
(Hertford)

Hartley [Anglo-Saxon]
'Meadow of the hart deer'.

Hartman [Teutonic]
'Strong and austere'. The original stoic. Also 'Keeper of the stags' (Anglo-Saxon).
(Hartmann)

Hartwell [Anglo-Saxon]
'Well where the deer drink'.
(Harwell, Hartwill, Harwill, Hart)

Hartwood [Anglo-Saxon]
'Forest of the hart deer'.
(Harwood)

Harvey [Teutonic/French]
'Army warrior' (Teutonic) or 'Bitter' (French).
(Hervey, Harve, Harv, Herve, Herv)

Haslett [Anglo-Saxon]
'Hazel tree grove on the headland'.
(Haslitt, Hazlett, Hazlitt)

Hastings [Anglo-Saxon]
'Son of violence'.

Havelock [Norse]
'Sea battle'.
(Havlock)

Haven [Anglo-Saxon]
'A place of safety'.

Hawley [Anglo-Saxon]
'From the hedged meadow'.

Hayden [Teutonic]
'From the hedged valley'.
(Haydon)

Hayward [Anglo-Saxon]
'Keeper of the hedged field'.
(Heyward)

Haywood [Anglo-Saxon]
'From the hedged forest'.
(Heywood)

Heath [Anglo-Saxon]
'Heathland'.

Heathcliff [Anglo-Saxon]
'From the heather cliff'.
(Heathcliffe)

Hector [Greek]
'Steadfast, unswerving; holds fast'.
(Eachan, Eachann, Eachunn, Heck)

Henry [Teutonic]
'Ruler of the estate'. Lord of the Manor.
(Hamlin, Heinrich, Heinrick, Hendrick, Henri, Henrik, Eanruig, Hanraoi, Harry, Hal, Hank)

Herald See **Harold**

Herbert [Teutonic]
'Brilliant warrior'.
(Harbert, Hebert, Hoireabard, Herb, Herbie, Bert)

Herman [Teutonic]
'Army warrior'.
(Harman, Harmon, Hermann, Ermin, Armand, Herm, Hermie, Armin, Armond, Armyn, Hermon)

Hernando See **Ferdinand**

Herrick [Teutonic]
' Army ruler'.

Hervey See **Harvey**

Hewe See **Hugh**

Hewett [Anglo-Saxon]
' Little Hugh'.

Heywood See **Haywood**

Herwin [Teutonic]
' Lover of war; battle companion'.

Hezekiah [Hebrew]
' God is strength'. Belief in God arms this man against all adversity.

Hiatt See **Hyatt**

Hilary [Latin]
' Cheerful and merry'.
(Hillary, Hillery Hilaire)

Hildebrand [Teutonic]
' Sword of war'.

Hilliard [Teutonic]
' War guardian; brave in battle'.
(Hillier, Hillyer)

Hilton [Anglo-Saxon]
' From the hill farm'.
(Hylton)

Hiram [Hebrew]
' Most noble and exalted one'.
(Hyram, Hi, Hy)

Hobart [Teutonic]
' Noble brilliance'.

Hogan [Celtic]
' Youth'.

Holbrook [Anglo-Saxon]
' From the brook in the valley'.

Holcomb [Anglo-Saxon]
' Deep valley'.
(Holcombe, Holecomb, Holecombe)

Holden [Anglo-Saxon/Teutonic]
'From the valley' or 'Kind'

Holgate [Anglo-Saxen]
'Gatekeeper'.

Hollis [Anglo-Saxon]
' Dweller in the holly grove '.

Holmes [Anglo-Saxon]
' From the island in the river'.

Holt [Anglo-Saxon]
' From the forest'.

Homer [Greek]
' A pledge'.

Horace [Latin]
' Time keeper; hours of the sun'.
(Horatio, Horatius, Race)

Horton [Anglo-Saxon]
' From the grey farm'.

Houghton [Anglo-Saxon]
' From the estate on the cliff'.

Hosea [Hebrew]
' Salvation'.

Houston [Anglo-Saxon]
' From the town in the mountains'.

Howard [Anglo-Saxon]
'Chief guardian'.
(Howie)

Howe [Teutonic]
'The eminent one'. A personage of high birth.

Howell [Celtic]
'Little, alert one'.
(Hywel, Hywell)

Howland [Anglo-Saxon]
'Dweller on the hill'.

Hubert [Teutonic]
'Brilliant, shining mind'.
(Hobart, Hubbard, Hoyt, Hugh, Hube, Bert, Hoibeard, Hugo, Hughes, Huey, Hughy, Hughie, Aodh, Aoidh)

Hudson [Anglo-Saxon]
'Son of the hoodsman'.

Hugh/Hugo See Hubert

Hulbert [Teutonic]
'Graceful'.
(Hulbard, Hulburd, Hulburt)

Humbert [Teutonic]
'Brilliant Hun' or 'Bright home'.
(Umberto, Humbie, Bert, Bertie, Berty)

Humphrey [Teutonic]
'Protector of the peace'.
(Humfrey, Humfry, Hump, Humph)

Hunter [Anglo-Saxon]
'A hunter'.
(Hunt)

Huntingdon [Anglo-Saxon]
'Hill of the hunter'.

Huntington [Anglo-Saxon]
'Hunting estate'.

Huntly [Anglo-Saxon]
'From the hunter's meadow .
(Huntley)

Hurlbert [Teutonic]
'Brilliant army leader'.

Hurley [Gaelic]
'Sea tide'.

Hurst [Anglo-Saxon]
'One who lives in the forest'.
(Hearst)

Hutton [Anglo-Saxon]
'From the farm on the ridge'.

Huxford [Anglo-Saxon]
'Hugh's Ford'.

Huxley [Anglo-Saxon]
'Hugh's meadow'.

Hyde [Anglo-Saxon]
'From the hide of land'. An old unit of measurement of land.

Hyatt [Anglo-Saxon]
'From the high gate'.
(Hiatt)

Hyman [Hebrew]
'Life'. The divine spark.

Hywel See Howell
(Hymen, Hymie, Hy)

Girls

Ianthe [Greek]
  ' Violet coloured flower '.
  (Iantha, Ianthina, Ian, Janthina, Janthine)

Ida [Teutonic]
  ' Happy '. Name comes from Mount Ida in Crete, where Jupiter is supposed to have been hidden.
  (Idalia, Idaline, Idalina, Idelea, Idelia, Idalia, Idella, Idalle, Idelle)

Idelia [Teutonic]
  ' Noble '.

Iduna [Norse]
  ' Lover '. The keeper of the golden apples of youth.
  (Idonia, Idonie)

Ierne [Latin]
  ' From Ireland '.

Ignatia [Latin]
  ' Fiery ardour '. Fem. of Ignatius.

Ila [French]
  ' From the island '.
  (Ilde)

Ileana [Greek]
  ' Of Ilion (Troy)'.

85

Ilka [Slavic]
'Flattering'.

Ilona See **Helen**

Ilse See **Elizabeth**

Imogene [Latin]
'Image of her mother'.
(Imogen)

Imperial [Latin]
'Imperial one'.

Inez See **Agnes**

Ingrid [Norse]
'Hero's daughter'. Child of a warrior.
(Inga, Inger, Ingunna, Inga-berg, Ingeborg, Ingebiorg, Ingibiorg)

Iniga [Latin]
'Fiery ardour'.
(Ignatia)

Iola [Greek]
'Colour of the dawn cloud'.
(Iole)

Iolanthe [Greek]
'Violet flower'.
(Yolanda, Yolande)

Ione [Greek]
'Violet coloured stone'.
(Iona)

Irene [Greek]
'Peace'. The Goddess of Peace.
(Eirene, Eirena, Erena, Irena, Irina, Irenna, Renata, Rena, Rene, Reini, Rennie, Renny)

Ireta [Latin]
'Enraged one'.
(Iretta, Irette, Irete)

Iris [Greek]
'The rainbow'. The messenger of the Gods.

Irma [Latin or Teutonic]
'Noble person' (Latin); 'Strong' (Teutonic).
(Erma, Erme, Irmina, Irmine, Irme)

Irvette [English]
'Sea friend'.
(Irvetta)

Isa [Teutonic]
'Lady of the iron will'. A determined lass.

Isabel [Hebrew]
Spanish form of Elizabeth, *q.v.*
(Isabella, Isabelle, Isobel, Isbel, Ishbel, Ysabel, Isabeau, Ysabeau, Ysobel, Ysabella, Ysabelle, Ysobella, Ysobelle, Bella, Belle, Bel) and the variations of Elizabeth

Isadora [Greek]
'The gift of Isis'.
(Isidora, Isidore, Isadore, Dora, Dori, Dory, Issie, Issy, Izzy)

Isis [Egyptian]
'Supreme goddess'. The Goddess of Fertility.

Isleen See **Aisleen**

Isolde [Celtic]
'The fair one'.
(Isoda, Ysolda, Ysolde, Yseult, Iseult, Eysllt)

Isola [Latin]
'The isolated one'. A
'loner'.

Isolabella [Combination
Isola/Bella]
'Beautiful lonely one'.
(Isolabelle)

Ita [Caelic]
'Desire for truth'.
(Ite)

Iva [French]
'The yew tree'.
(Ivanna, Ivanne)

Ivy [English]
'A vine'. The sacred plant
of the ancient religions.

Ian [Celtic]
'God is gracious'. See also John.
(Iain, Iaian)

Ichabod [Hebrew]
'The glory has departed'.

Ignatius [Latin]
'The ardent one'. A fiery patriot.
(Ignace, Ignate, Ignacio, Ignatius)

Igor [Scandinavian]
'The hero'.

Illtyd [Welsh]

Immanuel See Emmanuel

Inger [Norse]
'A son's army'.
(Ingar, Ingvar)

Ingemar [Norse]
'Famous son'.
(Ingmar)

Inglebert [Teutonic]
'Brilliant angel'.
(Englebert, Engelbert)

Ingram [Teutonic]
'The raven' or 'The raven's son'.
(Ingraham)

Inness [Celtic]
'From the island in the river'.
(Innes, Innis, Iniss)

Ira [Hebrew]
'The watcher'.

Irving [Anglo-Saxon/Celtic]
'Sea friend' (Anglo-Saxon) or 'White river' (Welsh/Celtic)
(Irvin, Irvine, Irwin, Erwin)

Isaac [Hebrew]
'The laughing one'.
(Isaak, Izaak, Ike, Ikey, Ikie)

Isham [Anglo-Saxon]
'From the estate of the iron man'.

Isidore [Greek]
'The gift of Isis'.
(Isidor, Isador, Isadore, Issy, Iz, Izzy, Izzie)

Israel [Hebrew]
'The Lord's soldier'. The warrior of god.
(Issie, Izzie)

Ivan See John

Ivar [Norse]
'Battle archer'. The warrior with the long bow.
(Iver, Ivor, Ives, Ivon, Ivo, Ives, Iven)

Ives [Anglo-Saxon]
'Son of the archer' or der. of Ivar.

Girls

Jacinda [Greek]
   ' Beautiful and comely '. Also
a var. of Hyacinth.
   (Jacenta)

Jacinth See **Hyacinth**

Jacoba [Latin]
   ' The supplanter '. The under-
study who is better than the
star.
   (Jacobina, Jacobine)

Jacqueline [Hebrew]
   ' The supplanter '.
   (Jacqueleine, Jacquelyn, Jac-
quetta, Jacketta, Jackelyn,
Jackeline, Jackie, Jacky)

Jade [Spanish]
   ' Daughter '. A mother's most
precious jewel.

Jane [Hebrew]
   ' God's gift of grace '. With
Mary the most consistently
popular girl's name, defying
fashion and whim. A selection
of variations:
   (Jan, Jana, Janet, Janette,
Janetta, Janice, Janina, Janna,
Jayne, Jean, Jeanne, Jeann-
ette, Jeanette, Jenette, Joan,
Joana, Joanna, Joanne, Jo-
hanna, Johanne, Juana, Juan-
ita, Sinead, Shena, Sheena,

Sine, Sean, Seon, Seonaid)

Janthina See Ianthe

Jarvia [Teutonic]
' Keen as a spear '.

Jasmin [Persian]
' Fragant flower '.
*(Jasmina, Jasmine, Jessamine,
Jessamyn, Jessamy, Jessamie,
Yasmin, Yasmina)*

Jayne [Sanskrit]
' God's victorious smile '.
Also a var. of Jane.

Jean See Jane

Jemina [Hebrew]
' The dove '. Symbol of peace.
(Jemie, Jemmie, Mina)

Jennifer See Guinevere

Jeremia [Hebrew]
' The Lord's exalted '. Fem.
of Jeremiah.
(Jeri, Jeri, Jerrie, Jerry)

Jeri See Geraldine or Jeremia

Jerusha [Hebrew]
' The married one '. The per-
fect wife.
(Yerusha)

Jessamine See Jasmine

Jessica [Hebrew]
' The rich one '.

Jewel [Latin]
' Most precious one '. The
ornament of the home.

Jill See Julia or Gillian

Jinx [Latin]
' Charming spell '. One who

can enchant with her beauty
and grace.
(Jynx)

Joan See Jane

Joakima [Hebrew]
' The Lord's Judge '.
(Joachima)

Jobina [Hebrew]
' The afflicted '. Fem. of Job.
(Jobyna)

Jocelyn [Latin]
' Fair and just '. Fem. of
Justin.
*(Jocelyne, Joceline, Jocelin,
Joscelyn, Joscelyne, Joscelin,
Josceline, Joslin, Josline, Jose-
lin, Joseline, Joselyn, Jose-
lyne, Joselen, Joselene, Josilin,
Josiline, Josilyn, Josilyne,
Josilen, Josilene, Justine, Jus-
tina, Lyn, Lynne)*

Joccoaa [Latin]
' The humour one '. Girl with
a lively wit.

Jody See Judith

Johanna See Jane

Jolie [French]
' Pretty '.

Joletta See Julia

Jordana [Hebrew]
' The descending '.

Josephine [Hebrew]
' She shall add '. Fem. of
Joseph.
*(Josepha, Josephina, Joette,
Josette, Josetta, Jo, Josie, Fifi,
Yusepha, Yosepha)*

Jovita [Latin]
 ' The joyful one '. The fem.
 of Jove the bringer of jollity.

Joyce [Latin]
 ' Gay and joyful '.
 (Joy, Joice, Joyous, Joycelyn,
 Joicelin, Joicelyn, Joycelin)

Juanita See **Jane**

Judith [Hebrew]
 ' Admired, praised '. One
 whose praises cannot be suffi-
 ciently rung.
 (Juditha, Judie, Judy, Jodie,
 Judy, Siobhan, Siuban)

Julia [Greek]
 ' Youthful '. Young in heart
 and mind.
 (Julie, Juliana, Juliane, Juli-
 anna, Julianne, Juliet, Juli-
 etta, Julina, Juline, Jill, Juli,
 Sile, Sileas)

June [Latin]
 ' Summer's child '. One born
 in the early summer.
 (Juna, Junia, Juniata, Junette,
 Junine, Juana)

Juno [Latin]
 ' Heavenly being '. The wife
 Jupiter, ruler of the heavens.

Justine See **Jocelyn**

Jabez [Hebrew]
' Cause of sorrow '.

Jack See **John**

Jacob [Hebrew]
'The supplanter'.
(Jacobus, Jacques, Jamie, Jim, Jimmie, Jimmy, Jas, Hamish, Diego, Seamus, Shamus, Jem, Jemmie, Jemmy, Jock, Jocko)

Jagger [Northumbrian]
' A carter '.

James See **Jacob**

Jared [Hebrew]
' The descendant '.

Jarman [Teutonic]
' The German '.
(Jerman)

Jarvis See **Gervase**

Jason [Greek]
' The healer '.

Jasper See **Gaspar**

Javier See **Xavier**

Jay [Anglo-Saxon]
' Jay or crow '. Also used as dim. for any name beginning with J.

Jedediah [Hebrew]
' Beloved by the Lord '.
(Jed, Jedidiah, Jeddy)

Jeffrey See **Geoffrey**

Jefferson [Anglo-Saxon]
' Jeffrey's son '.

Jeremy [Hebrew]
' Exalted by the Lord '.

(Jeremiah, Jeremias, Jerry)

Jermyn See **Jarman**

Jerome [Latin]
' Sacred; holy '. A man of God.
(Jerome, Gerome, Jerry)

Jerrold See **Gerald**

Jervis See **Gervase**

Jervoise See **Gervase**

Jesse [Hebrew]
' God's gift '.
(Jess)

Jethro [Hebrew]
' Excellent; without equal '.

Jevon See **John**

Joachim [Hebrew]
'Judgement of the Lord'.

Job [Hebrew]
' The persecuted; the afflicted '.

Jock See **John/James**

Joel [Hebrew]
' The Lord is God '.
(Joe, Joey)

John [Hebrew]
' God's gracious gift '. The most consistently popular boy's name.
(Jon, Jean, Jack, Jock, Jevon, Jan, Johan, Johann, Jackie, Johnnie, Johnny, Sean, Shawn, Shane, Sian, Evan, Ivan, Ian, Gian, Hans,

Zane, Iain, Iaian, Eoin, Seain, Seann)

Jonah [Hebrew]
' Peace '.

Jonas [Hebrew]
' Dove '. A man of peace and tranquillity.

Jonathan [Hebrew]
' Gift of the Lord '.
(Jon)

Jordan [Hebrew]
' The descending river '.
(Jordon, Jourdain)

Joseph [Hebrew]
' He shall add '.
(Joe, Joey, Jose, Isoep, Seosaidh, Josiah)

Joshua [Hebrew]
' God's salvation '. A man saved by his belief in God.
(Josh)

Jotham [Hebrew]
' God is perfect '.

Judd [Hebrew]
'Praised; extolled '.
(Judah)

Julius [Latin]
' Youthful shaveling '.
(Jules, Julian, Joliet, Jule, Julie)

Junius [Latin]
' Born in June '.

Justin [Latin]
' The just one '. One of upright principles and morals.
(Justus, Just)

Justis [French]
' Justice '. A strict upholder of the moral laws.

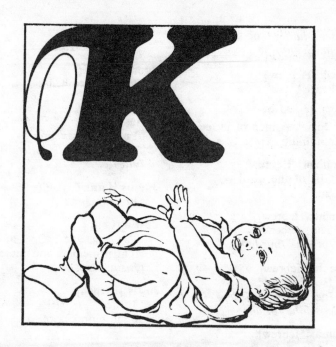

Girls

Kama [Sanskrit]
'Love'. The Hindu god of love, equivalent to Cupid.

Kara See **Cara**

Karen See **Katherine**

Kasmira [Slavic]
'Commands peace'.
(Casmira)

Katherine [Greek]
'Pure maiden'. Another spelling of Catherine.
(Katharine, Katharina, Katherina, Katheryn, Kathryn, Katrin, Katrina, Katryn, Kathleen, Kathlene, Kitty, Katie, Kathie, Kay, Kate, Kara, Karen, Karena, Karin, Karyn and all var. of Catherine)

Keely [Gaelic]
'The beautiful one'.

Kelda [Norse]
'Bubbling spring'.
(Kelly)

Kerridwen *See Ceiridwen*

Kerry [Gaelic]
'Dark one'.
(Kerri)

Ketti See **Katherine**

Ketura [Hebrew]
' Incense '.

Kevin [Gaelic]
' Gentle and lovable '.
(Kelvina)

Kim [Origin not known]
' Noble chief '.

Kimberley [English]
' From the royal meadow '.
Popular in Victorian/Edwardian times following the Relief of Kimberley.

Kineta [Greek]
' Active and elusive '.

Kirstin [Norse]
' The annointed one '.
(Kirstina, Kirstie, Kirsty)

Koren [Greek]
' Beautiful maiden '.

Kyna [Gaelic]
' Great wisdom '.

Kane [Celtic]
'Little, warlike one' or 'Radiant brightness'.

Karl See **Charles**

Karney See **Kearney**

Karr See **Carr**

Kaspar See **Gaspar**

Kavan See **Cavan**

Kay [Celtic]
'Rejoiced in'. Also dim. for any name beginning with K.

Keane [Anglo-Saxon]
'Bold and handsome'. A sharp witted man.

Kedar [Arabic]
'Powerful'.

Keefe [Celtic]
'Handsome, noble and admirable'.

Keegan [Celtic]
'Little fiery one'.

Keelan [Celtic]
'Little slender one'.

Keeley [Celtic]
'Little, handsome one'.

Keenan [Celtic]
'Little ancient one'.

Keith [Celtic]
'A place' or 'From the forest' (Welsh).

Kell [Norse]
'From the well'.

Keller [Gaelic]
'Little companion'.

Kelly [Gaelic]
'The warrior'.
(Kelley)

Kelsey [Norse/Teutonic]
'Dweller on the island' (Norse) or 'From the water'. (Teutonic).

Kelvin [Gaelic]
'From the narrow stream'.
(Kelvan, Kelven)

Kemp [Anglo-Saxon]
'The warrior champion'.

Kendall [Celtic]
'Chief of the valley'.
(Kendal, Kendell, Ken)

Kendrick [Gaelic/Anglo-Saxon]
'Son of Henry' (Gaelic) or 'Royal ruler' (Anglo-Saxon)

Kenelm [Anglo-Saxon]
'Brave helmet'. A courageous protector.

Kenley [Anglo-Saxon]
'Owner of a royal meadow'.

Kenn [Celtic]
'Clear as bright water'.

Kennard [Anglo-Saxon]
'Bold and vigorous'.

Kennedy [Gaelic]
'The helmeted chief'.

Kenneth [Celtic]
'The handsome' or 'Royal oath'.
(Keneth, Kennet, Ken, Kenny, Kent)

Kenrick [Anglo-Saxon]
' Bold ruler '.

Kent [Celtic]
' Bright and white '. Also dim.
of Kenneth.

Kenton [Anglo-Saxon]
' From the royal estate '.

Kenward [Anglo-Saxon]
' Bold guardian '.

Kenway [Anglo-Saxon]
' Bold or royal warrior '.

Kenyon [Celtic]
' White haired '.

Kermit [Celtic]
' A free man '.
(Dermot, Derry, Kerry)

Kern [Gaelic]
' Little dark one '.

Kerr See **Carr**

Kerry [Gaelic]
' Son of the dark one '.

Kerwin [Gaelic]
' Small black haired one '.

Kester [Anglo-Saxon]
' From the army camp '. Also
used as dim. of Christopher.

Kevin [Gaelic]
' Gentle, kind and lovable '.
(Kevan, Keven, Kev)

Key [Gaelic]
' Son of the fiery one '.

Kieran [Gaelic]
' Small and dark skinned '.
(Kieron, Kerrin, Kerry)

Killian [Gaelic]
' Little warlike one '.

Kimball [Celtic]
' Royally brave ' or ' Warrior
chief '.
*(Kimble, Kimbell, Kemble,
Kim)*

King [Anglo-Saxon]
' The sovereign '. The ruler of
his people.

Kingsley [Anglo-Saxon]
' From the king's meadow '.

Kingston [Anglo-Saxon]
' From the king's farm '.

Kingswell [Anglo-Saxon]
' From the king's well '.

Kinnard [Gaelic]
' From the high mountain '.
(Kinnaird)

Kinnell [Gaelic]
' Dweller on the top of the
cliff '.

Kinsey [Anglo-Saxon]
' Royal victor '.

Kipp [Anglo-Saxon]
' Dweller on the pointed hill '.

Kirby [Teutonic]
' From the church village '.
(Kerby, Kerr)

Kirk [Norse]
' Dweller at the church '.

Kirkley [Anglo-Saxon]
' From the church meadow '.

Kirkwood [Anglo-Saxon]
' From the church wood '.

Kirwin See **Kerwin**

Kit See **Christopher**

Knight [Anglo-Saxon]
' Mounted soldier '.

Knox [Anglo-Saxon]
' From the hills '.

Knut See **Canute**

Konrad See **Conrad**

Kurt See **Conrad/Curtis**

Kynan See **Conan**

Kyle [Gaelic]
' From the strait '.

Kyne [Anglo-Saxon]
' The royal one '.

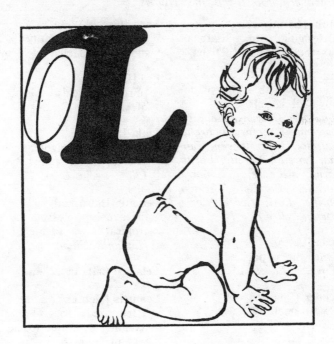

Girls

Lala [Slavic]
' The tulip flower '.

Lalage [Greek]
'Gentle laughter'

Lalita [Sanskrit]
' Without guile '.

Lana See Alana

Lanette [French]
(Lanetta)

Lani [Hawaiian]
' The sky '.

Lara [Latin]
' Famous '.

Laraine See Lorraine

Larissa [Greek]
' Cheerful maiden '. One who
is as happy as a lark.

Lark [English]
' Singing bird '.

La Roux [French]
' The red haired one '.
(Larousse)

Lasca [Latin]
' Weary one '.

Lassie [Scots]
' Little girl '.

Latonia [Latin]
' Belonging to Latona '. was the mother of Diana.

Laura [Latin]
' Laurel wreath '. The victor's crown of laurels.
(Laurel, Lauren, Laureen, Laurena, Laurene, Lauretta, Laurette, Lora, Loren, Lorena, Loretta, Lorette, Lorita, Lorna, Laure, Lorenza, Loralie, Lorelie, Lorinda, Lorine, Lori, Loree, Lorie, Lorrie, Laurie)

Laveda [Latin]
' One who is purified '.
(Lavetta, Lavette)

Lavender [English]
' Sweet smelling flower '.
(Lavvie)

Laverne [French]
' Spring like ' or ' Alder tree '.
(Laverna, Verna, Verne, Vern)

Lavinia [Latin]
' Lady of Rome '.
(Lavina, Vina, Vinia)

Leah [Hebrew]
' The weary one '.
(Lea, Lee, Leigh)

Leala [French]
' The true one '. One who is true to home, family and friends.

Leatrice [Combination Leah/Beatrice]
' Tired but joyful '.
(Leatrix)

Leda [Greek]
' Mother of beauty '. The mother of Helen of Troy.

Lee [English]
' From the fields '. Also a var. of Leah.

Leila [Arabic]
' Black as the night '.
(Leilia, Lela, Lilia, Leilah, Lilah, Leela, Lee)

Leilani [Hawaiian]
' Heavenly blossom '. The tropical flower of the Islands.
(Lullani, Lillani)

Lela See **Leila** or **Lilian**

Lemuela [Hebrew]
' Dedicated to God '. A daughter dedicated to the service of God.
(Lemuella)

Lena [Latin]
' Enchanting one '. Also a dim. of Caroline, Madeleine, Helena.
(Lina)

Lenis [Latin]
' Smooth and white as the lily .'
(Lene, Lenta, Lenita, Leneta, Lenos)

Leoda [Teutonic]
' Woman of the people '.
(Leola)

Leoma [Anglo-Saxon]
' Bright light'. One who casts radiance around her.

Leona [Latin]
' The lioness '.
*(Leola, Leonie, Leone, Leoni,
Lennie, Lenny)*

Leonarda [French]
' Like a lion '.
*(Leonarde, Leonardina,
Leonardine)*

Leonora See **Eleanor**

Leontine [Latin]
' Like the lion '.
(Leontina, Leontyne)

Leopoldina [Teutonic]
' The people's champion '.
Fem. of Leopold.
(Leopoldine, Leopolda)

Leota See **Leoda**

Lesley [Celtic]
' Keeper of the grey fort '.
(Leslie, Lesli, Lesly, Les)

Leta See **Letitia**

Letha [Greek]
' Sweet oblivion '. Lethe the
river of forgetfulness.
*(Lethia, Lethitha, Leithia,
Leda, Leta)*

Letitia [Latin]
' Joyous gladness '.
*(Laetitia, Leticia, Letizia,
Lettice, Lettie, Leta, Leda,
Tish)*

Levana [Latin]
' The sun of the dawn '. The
Goddess of childbirth.
(Levania)

Levina [English]
' A bright flash '. One who
passes like a comet.

Lewanna [Hebrew]
' As pure as the white moon '.
(Luanna)

Lexine See **Alexandra**

Leya [Spanish]
' Loyalty to the law '. A strict
upholder of morals and principles.

Liana [French]
' The climbing vine '.
*(Leane, Leana, Leanna,
Lianna, Lianne)*

Libby See **Elizabeth**

Lila See **Leila**

Lilac [Persian]
' Dark mauve flower '.

Lilian [Latin]
' A lily '. One who is pure in
thought, word and deed.
*(Lillian, Liliana, Lilliana,
Liliane, Lilliane, Lilyan,
Lillyan, Lily, Lili, Lilli, Lilly,
Lilias, Lilais, Lillis, Lela,
Lelah, Lelia, Leila, Lila,
Lilah, Lilia, Lilla)*

Lilith [Arabic]
' Woman of the night '.
According to Eastern belief,
Lilith was the first wife of
Adam and the first woman in
the world; Eve was his
second wife.

Linda [Spanish]
' Pretty one '. Also dim. of Belinda, Rosalinda, etc.
(Lind, Linde, Lindie, Lindy, Lynda, Lynd)

Linnea [Norse]
' The lime blossom '.

Linnet [French]
' Sweet bird '.
(Linnette, Linette, Linetta, Linnetta, Lynette, Lynnette)

Lisa See **Elizabeth**

Lodema [English]
' Leader or guide '.

Lois See **Louise**

Lola [Spanish]
' Strong woman '.
(Loleta, Lolita, Lollie)

Lona [Anglo-Spanish]
' Solitary watcher '.

Lora See **Laura**

Lorelei [Teutonic]
' Siren of the river '. The Rhine maiden who lured unwary mariners to their deaths.
(Lorelie, Lorelia)

Lorena/Loretta See **Laura**

Lorna See **Laura**

Lorraine [Teutonic or French]
' Renowned in battle ' (Teutonic); ' The Queen '
(French).
(Loraine, Laraine, Larraine, Larayne)

Lotus [Greek]
' Flower of the sacred Nile '

Louella See **Luella**

Louise [Teutonic]
' Famous battle maid '. One who leads victorious armies into battle.
(Louisa, Luise, Lois, Loise, Louisitte, Labhaoise, Liusade, Loyce, Eloise, Eloisa, Heloise, Aloisa, Aloisia, Aloysia, Alison, Allison)

Love [English]
' Tender affection '.

Luana [Teutonic]
' Graceful army maiden '.
(Luane, Louanna, Louanne, Luwana, Luwanna, Luwanne)

Lucianna [Combination
Lucy/Anne]

Lucille/Lucinda See **Lucy**

Lucretia [Latin]
' A rich reward '.
(Lucrezia, Lucrece, Lucrecia)

Lucy [Latin]
' Light '. One who brings the lamp of learning to the ignorant.

Ludella [Angla-Saxon]
' Pixie maid '.

Ludmilla [Slavic]
' Beloved of the people '.
(Ludmila)

Luella [Anglo-Saxon]
' The appeaser '.
(Louella, Loella, Luelle)

Lunetta [Latin]
' Little Moon '.
(Luna, Luneta)

Lupe [Spanish]
' She wolf '. A fierce guardian
of the home.

Lurline [Teutonic]
' Siren '. A version of Lorelie.
*(Lurlina, Lura, Lurleen, Lur-
lene, Lurlette)*

Luvena [Latin]
' Little beloved one '.

Lydia [Greek]
' Cultured one '.
(Lidia, Lydie, Lidie)

Lynn [Celtic]
' A waterfall '. Also dim. of
Carolyn, Evelyn, etc.
(Lynne)

Lyris [Greek]
' She who plays the harp '.
(Lyra)

Lysandra [Greek]
' The Liberator '. The proto-
type of Women's Lib!

Laban [Hebrew]
' White '.

Lach [Celtic]
' Dweller by the water '.
(Lache)

Lachlan [Celtic]
' The warlike '.

Lacy [Latin]
' From the Roman manor house '.

Laibrook [Anglo-Saxon]
' Path by the brook '.

Ladd [Anglo-Saxon]
' Attendant; page '.
(Laddie)

Laidley [Anglo-Saxon]
' From the water meadow '.

Laird [Celtic]
' The land owner '. The lord of the manor.

Lamar [Teutonic]
' Famous throughout the land '.

Lambert [Teutonic]
' Rich in land '. An owner of vast estates.

Lamont [Norse]
' A lawyer '.
(Lamond, Lammond, Lammont)

Lancelot [French]
' Spear attendant '.
(Launcelot, Launce, Lancey, Lance)

Lander [Anglo-Saxon]
' Owner of a grassy plain '.
(Launder, Landor, Landers)

Landon [Anglo-Saxon]
' Dweller on the long hill '.
(Langdon, Langston)

Lane [Anglo-Saxon]
' From the narrow road '.

Lang [Teutonic]
' Tall or long limbed man '.

Langdon See **Landon**

Langford [Anglo-Saxon]
' Dweller by the long ford '.

Langley [Anglo-Saxon]
' Dweller by the long meadow '.

Langston [Anglo-Saxon]
' The farm belonging to the tall man '.

Langworth [Anglo-Saxon]
' From the long enclosure '.

Lars See **Lawrence**

Larson [Norse]
' Son of Lars '.

Latham [Norse]
' From the barns '.

Lathrop [Anglo-Saxon]
' From the barn farmstead '.

Latimer [Anglo-Saxon]
' The interpreter; the language teacher '.

Lawford [Anglo-Saxon]
' Dweller at the ford by the hill '.

Lawler [Gaelic]
' The mumbler '.

Lawley [Anglo-Saxon]
' From the meadow on the hill '.

Lawrence [Latin]
'Crowned with laurels'. The victor's crown of bay leaves.
(Laurence, Larrance, Lawrance, Lorenz, Laurent, Lars, Larry, Lauren, Laurie, Lawry, Loren, Lorin, Lon, Lonnie, Lorenzo, Lori, Lorrie, Lorry, Lauritz, Labhras, Labhruinn)

Lawson [Anglo-Saxon]
'Son of Lawrence'

Lawton [Anglo-Saxon]
'From the town on the hill'.

Lazarus See **Eleazar**

Leal [Anglo-Saxon]
'Loyal, true and faithful'.

Leander [Greek]
'The lion man'.

Lee [Anglo-Saxon/Gaelic]
'From the meadow' (Anglo-Saxon) or 'Poetic' (Gaelic).
(Leigh)

Leggett [French]
'Envoy or ambassador'.
(Leggitt, Liggett)

Leicester See **Lester**

Leif [Norse]
'The beloved one'.

Leigh See **Lee**

Leighton [Anglo-Saxon]
'Dweller at the farm by the meadow'.
(Layton)

Leith [Celtic]
'Broad, wide river'.

Leland [Anglo-Saxon]
'Dweller by the meadow land'.
(Leyland, Lealand)

Lemuel [Hebrew]
'Consecrated to God'.
(Lem, Lemmie)

Lenard See **Leonard**

Lennon [Gaelic]
'Little cloak'.

Lennox [Celtic]
'Grove of elm trees'.

Leo [Latin]
'Lion'.

Leon [French]
'Lion-like'.

Leonard [Latin]
'Lion brave'. One with all the courage and tenacity of the king of beasts.
(Leoner, Lennard, Lenard, Leonhard, Len, Lennie, Lenny)

Leopold [Teutonic]
'Brave for the people'. One who fights for his countrymen.
(Leo, Lepp)

Leroy [French]
'The king'.
(Lee, Roy)

Leslie [Celtic]
'From the grey fort'.
(Lesley, Les)

Lester [Anglo-Saxon]
'From the army camp'.

Leverett [French]
'The young hare'.

Leverton [Anglo-Saxon]
'From the rush farm'.

Levi [Hebrew]
'United'.

Lewis [Teutonic]
'Famous battle warrior'.
(Louis, Ludwig, Lewes, Ludovic, Ludovick, Lugaidh, Luthais, Lou, Lew, Ludo)

Liam See **William**

Lincoln [Celtic]
'From the place by the pool'.

Lind [Anglo-Saxon]
'From the lime tree'.
(Linden, Lyndon)

Lindberg [Teutonic]
'Lime tree hill'.

Lindell [Anglo-Saxon]
'Dweller by the lime tree in the valley'.

Lindley [Anglo-Saxon]
'By the lime tree in the meadow'.

Lindon See **Lind**

Lindsey [Anglo-Saxon]
'Pool island'.
(Lindsay, Linsay, Linsey)

Linford [Anglo-Saxon]
'From the lime tree ford'.

Link [Anglo-Saxon]
'From the bank or edge'.

Linley [Anglo-Saxon]
'From the flax field'.

Linn See **Lynn**

Linton [Anglo-Saxon]
'From the flax farm'.

Linus [Greek]
'Flax coloured hair'.

Lionel [French]
'The young lion'.
(Lion)

Litton [Anglo-Saxon]
'Farm on the hillside'.

Llewellyn [Welsh]
'Lion like' or 'Like a ruler'.

Lloyd [Welsh]
'Grey-haired'.
(Floyd)

Locke [Anglo-Saxon]
'Dweller in the stronghold'.

Logan [Celtic]
'Little hollow'.

Lombard [Latin]
'Long bearded one'.

Lon [Gaelic]
'Strong, fierce'. Also dim. of Lawrence.

Loren See **Lawrence**

Loring [Teutonic]
'Man from Lorraine'.

Louis See **Lewis**

Lothar See **Luther**

Lowell [Anglo-Saxon]
'The beloved one'.
(Lovel, Lovell)

Loyal See **Leal**

Lucas See **Luke**

Lucius [Latin]
' Light '.
(Lucas, Luke, Lucian, Luck, Luc, Lukas, Lucais, Luce, Lukey)

Ludlow [Anglo-Saxon]
' From the hill of the prince '.

Ludwig See **Lewis**

Luke See **Lucius**

Lundy [French]
' Born on Monday '.

Lunn [Gaelic]
' From the grove '.

Lunt [Norse]
' Strong and fierce '.

Luther [Teutonic]
' Famous warrior '.
(Lothar, Lothaire, Lothario, Lute)

Lyle [French]
' From the island '.
(Lyall, Lyell, Lisle, Liall)

Lyman [Anglo-Saxon]
' Man from the meadow '.
(Leyman)

Lyndon See **Lind**

Lynn [Welsh]
' From the pool or waterfall '.
(Lyn, Lin, Linn)

Lysander [Greek]
' The liberator '.
(Sandy)

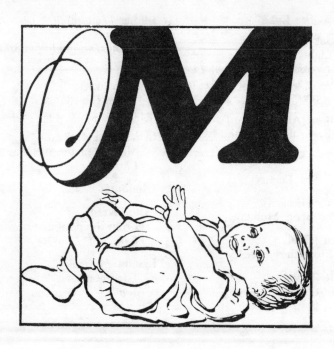

Girls

Mab [Gaelic]
'Mirthful joy'.

Mabel [Latin]
'Amiable and loving' An endearing companion.

Madora See **Medea**

Madeline [Greek]
'Tower of strength'. A woman of great physical and moral courage, on whom many could lean in difficult times.
(Madeleine, Madelaine, Madaline, Madaleine, Madalaine, Madalena, Maddalena, Maddalene, Madelon, Madlin, Madel, Madelia, Madella, *Madelle, Magdala, Magdaa, Magdalen, Magdalene, Magdalyn, Magdalane, Malena, Marleen, Marlene, Marline, Marlena, Malina, Mada, Madelle, Maddy, Mala)*

Madge See **Margaret**

Madra [Spanish]
'The matriarch'.

Mae See **May**

Maeve [Irish]
The warrior queen of Connaught
(Mave, Meave)

Magdalene See **Madeleine**

Maggie See **Margaret**

Magnilda [Teutonic]
' Great battle maid '.
*(Magnilde, Magnhilda,
Magnhilde, Mag, Maggie,
Nilda, Nillie)*

Magnolia [Latin]
' Magnolia flower '.
(Mag, Maggie, Nola, Nolie)

Mahala [Hebrew]
' Tenderness '.
(Mahalah, Mahalia)

Maia See **May**

Maida [Anglo-Saxon]
' The maiden '.
*(Maidie, Mady, Maidel, May-
da, Mayde, Maydena)*

Maisie See **Margaret**

Majesta [Latin]
' Majestic One '.

Malise [Gaelic]
'Servant of God'.

Malva [Greek]
' Soft and tender '.
(Melva, Melba)

Malvina [Gaelic]
' Polished chieftain '.
*(Malva, Melva, Melvina,
Malvie, Melvine)*

Manon See **Mary**

Manuela [Spanish]
' God with us '.
(Manuella)

Marcella [Latin]
' Belonging to Mars '.
*(Marcie, Marcy, Marcelle,
Marcelline, Marcelline, Mar-
cile, Marcille, Marcela, Mar-
celia, Marchella, Marchelle,
Marchelline, Marchita, Mar-
quita, Marsha, Marilda)*

Marelda [Teutonic]
' Famous battle maiden '.

Margaret [Latin]
' A pearl '.
*(Margareta, Margaretta, Mar-
garita, Margery, Margory,
Marjery, Marjorie, Margorie,
Margerie, Margharita, Mar-
get, Margette, Margetta, Mar-
galo, Marguerite, Margerita,
Margueritta, Marguerita,
Marfot, Margarethe, Mar-
gethe, Margaretha, Maigrgh-
read, Margo, Margao, Marge,
Maggie, Meta, Meg, Maisie,
Grete, Greta, Grethe, Gret-
chen, Peggy, Rita, Daisy)*

Marian [Hebrew]
' Bitter and graceful '.
*(Marion, Marianne, Mariana,
Marianna, Maryanne,
Mariam, Mariom)*

Marigold [English]
' Golden flower girl '.
(Marygold)

Marina [Latin]
' Lady of the sea '.

Mariposa [Spanish]
'Butterfly'

Marlene See **Madeleine**

Margery See **Margaret**

Marsha See **Marcella**

Martha [Arabic]
' The mistress '.
(Marta, Marthe, Martie,

Marty, Mattie, Matty, Martella)

Martina [Latin]
'Warlike one'. Fem. of Martin.
(Martine, Marta, Tina)

Marvel [Latin]
'A wondrous miracle'.
(Marva, Marvella, Marvela, Marvelle)

Mary [Hebrew]
'Bitterness'. Although Hebrew in origin has become one of the most consistently popular names for girls, since the Christian era.
(Mara, Maria, Marie, Maretta, Marette, Marilyn, Marylyn, Marilin, Marilla, Marla, Marya, Miriam, Mamie, Manette, Manon, Maryse, Maire, Maureen, Mearr, Moya, Mairi, Molly, May, Marietta, Polly, Mitzi, Mimi, Mariette)

Marylou [Combination Mary/Louise]

Mathilda [Teutonic]
'Brave little maid'. One as courageous as a lion.
(Matilda, Matilde, Mathilde, Maud, Maude, Mattie, Tilda, Tilly, Matelda, Maitilde)

Mattea [Hebrew]
'Gift of God'. Fem. of Matthew.
(Matthea, Matthia, Mathea, Mathia)

Maud See **Mathilda**

Maureen See **Mary**

Mauve [Latin]
'Lilac coloured bird'.
(Malva)

Mavis [French]
'Song thrush'.

Maxine [French]
'The greatest'. Fem. of Maximilian.
(Maxima, Maxene, Maxie)

May [Latin]
'Born in May'. Also dim. of Mary.

Maybelle See **Mabel**

Meara [Gaelic]
'Mirth'.

Medea [Greek]
'The middle child' or 'Enchantress'.
(Media, Madora, Medora)

Megan [Celtic]
'The strong'. Popular name for Welsh girls.
(Meghan)

Mehitabel [Hebrew]
'Favoured of God'. One of the Chosen.
(Mehetabel, Mehetabie, Mehetabelle, Mehitable, Mehitabelle, Metabel, Hetty, Hitty)

Melanie [Greek]
'Clad in darkness'. Lady of the night.
(Melania, Malan, Melan, Mel, Mellie, Melly, Melany)

Melantha [Greek]
'Dark flower'.
(Melanthe)

Melba See **Malva**

Melina [Latin]
' Yellow canary '. Also der.
of Madeline.

Melinda [Greek]
' Mild and gentle '. A quiet
home loving girl.
(Malinda)

Melissa [Greek]
' Honey bee '.
(Melisa, Lisa, Mel)

Melody [Greek]
' Like a song '.
(Melodie, Melodia, Lodie)

Melvina See **Malva**

Meriel See **Muriel**

Mercedes [Spanish]
' Compassionate, merciful '.
One who forgives, not con-
demns.
(Mercy, Merci)

Mercia [Anglo-Saxon]
' Lady of Mercia '. One
from the old Saxon kingdom
in the centre of England.

Meredith [Celtic]
' Protector from the sea '. A
popular name in Wales for
boys and girls.
*(Meridith, Meredyth, Meri-
dyth, Merideth, Meredeth,
Meredydd, Merrie, Merry)*

Merle [Latin]
' The blackbird '.
*(Merl, Merlina, Merline,
Meryl, Myrlene, Merola,
Merla)*

Merna See **Myrna**

Merrie [Anglo-Saxon]
' Mirthful, joyous '. Also dim.
of Meredith.
(Meri, Merri, Merry)

Merritt [Anglo-Saxon]
' Worthy; of merit '.
*(Meritt, Merrit, Meritta,
Merritta)*

Mertice [Anglo-Saxon]
' Famous and pleasant '. One
who has not been spoiled by
adulation.
(Merdyce, Mertyce)

Meryl See **Merle**

Messina [Latin]
' The middle child '.

Meta [Latin]
' Ambition achieved '.

Metis [Greek]
' Wisdom and skill '.
(Metys)

Michaela [Hebrew]
' Likeness to God '. Fem. of
Michael.
*(Michaelina, Michaeline, Mi-
cheline, Michelline, Micaela,
Mikaela, Michel, Michelle,
Michella, Michaella)*

Mignon [French]
' Little, dainty darling '. A
kitten-like creature of charm
and grace.
(Mignonette)

Mildred [Anglo-Saxon]
' Gentle counsellor '. The
diplomat power behind the
throne.
(Mildrid, Milli, Millie, Milly)

Millicent [Teutonic]
' Strong and industrious '.
The hard working chatelaine.
(Melicent, Melisande, Melli-
cent, Melisende, Melisanda,
Melisenda, Milicent, Milis-
sent, Milisent, Milli, Millie,
Milly)

Mimi See **Mary**

Mimosa [Latin]
'Imitative'

Minerva [Latin]
' Wise, purposeful one '. The
Goddess of Wisdom.

Minette [French]
' Little kitten '.
(Minetta)

Minta [Teutonic]
' Remembered with love '.
(Mina, Minda, Mindy, Min-
etta, Minnie)

Minta [Greek]
' The mint plant '. Also dim.
of Araminta.
(Minthe, Mintha)

Mira [Latin]
' Wonderful one '.
(Mirella, Mirilla)

Mirabel [Latin]
' Admired for her beauty '.
(Mirabella, Mirabelle)

Miranda [Latin]
' Greatly admired '.
(Randa)

Miriam See **Mary**

Mitzi See **Mary**

Modesty [Latin]
' Shy, modest '. The retiring

and bashful maiden.
(Modesta, Modeste, Modes-
tia, Modestine, Desta)

Moira See **Morag**

Monica [Latin]
' Advice giver '.
(Monique, Mona, Monca)

Morag [Celtic]
'Great'
(Moira, Moyra)

Morna See **Myrna**

Morgana [Welsh]
' From the sea shore '.
(Morgan)

Moselle [Hebrew]
' Taken from the water '.
Fem. of Moses.
(Mosella, Mozel, Mozelle,
Mozella)

Muriel [Celtic]
'Sea bright' *(Meriel, Muire)*

Musetta [French]
' Child of the Muses '.
(Musette)

Musidora [Greek]
' Gift of the Muses '.

Myfanwy [Welsh]

Myra [Latin]
'Admired' 'Wonderful one'.

Myrlene See **Merle**

Myrna [Gaelic]
'Beloved'.
(Merna, Mirna, Moina,
Morna, Moyna)

Myrtle [Greek]
' Victorious crown '. The
hero's laurel wreath.
(Myrta, Myrtia, Myrtis,
Mirle, Mertle, Mertice)

Mac [Celtic]
Used in many Scots and Irish names and meaning Son of: Also used in the form 'Mc'. For instance Macadam (Son of Adam), McDonald (Son of Donald) and so on.

Macy [French]
'From Matthew's estate'.

Maddock [Welsh]
'Beneficient'.
(Madoc, Madock, Madog, Maddox)

Madison [Anglo-Saxon]
'Mighty in battle'.
(Maddison)

Magee [Gaelic]
'Son of the fiery one'.

Magnus [Latin]
'The great one'. One who excels all others.

Maitland [Anglo-Saxon]
'Dweller in the meadow land'.

Major [Latin]
'Greater'. Anything you can do, he can do better!

Malcolm [Celtic]
'The dove' or 'Follower of St. Columba'.

Malin [Anglo-Saxon]
'Little warrior'.

Mallory [Anglo-Saxon/Latin]
'Army counsellor' (Anglo-Saxon) or 'Luckless' (Celtic).

Maloney [Gaelic]
'Believer in the Sabbath'.

Malvin [Celtic]
'Polished chief'.
(Melvin, Mal, Mel)

Mandel [Teutonic]
'Almond'.

Manfred [Anglo-Saxon]
'Peaceful hero'.
(Manfried)

Manley [Anglo-Saxon]
'The hero's meadow'
(Manleich)

Manning [Anglo-Saxon]
'Hero's son'.

Mansfield [Anglo-Saxon]
'Hero's field'.

Manton [Anglo-Saxon]
'Hero's farm'.

Manville [French]
'From the great estate'
(Manvil)

Manuel See **Emmanuel**

Marcel [Latin]
'Little follower of Mars'. A warlike person.
(Marcellus, Marcello)

Marcus See **Mark**

Marden [Anglo-Saxon]
'From the pool in the valley'.

Marion [French]
'Bitter'. A French form of Mary, often given as a boy's name in compliment to the Virgin.

Marius [Latin]
'The martial one'.
(Mario)

Mark [Latin]
'Follower of Mars; the warrior'.
(Marcus, Marco, Marc)

Marland [Anglo-Saxon]
'Dweller in the lake land'.

Marley [Anglo-Saxon]
'From the lake in the meadow'.
(Marly)

Marlon, Marlin See Merlin

Marlow [Anglo-Saxon]
'From the lake on the hill'.
(Marlowe)

Marmaduke [Celtic]
'Sea leader'.
(Duke)

Marmion [French]
'Very small one'.

Marsden [Anglo-Saxon]
'From the marshy valley'.
(Marsdon)

Marsh [Anglo-Saxon]
'From the marsh'.

Marshall [Anglo-Saxon]
'The steward'. The man who looked after the estate of a nobleman.

Marston [Anglo-Saxon]
'From the farm by the lake'.

Martin [Latin]
'Warlike person'. A follower of Mars.
(Marten, Marton, Mart, Martie, Marty)

Marvin [Anglo-Saxon]
'Famous friend'.

(Mervin, Merwin, Merwyn)

Marwood [Anglo-Saxon]
'From the lake in the forest'.

Maslin [French]
'Small Thomas'.
(Maslen, Maslon)

Mason [Latin]
'Worker in stone'. One who built castles, churches, houses, etc. from stone.

Mather [Anglo-Saxon]
'Powerful army'.

Matthew [Hebrew]
'Gift of God'. One of the 12 Apostles.
(Mathew, Mathias, Mattias, Mata, Matthias, Mat, Matt, Mattie, Matty)

Maurice [Latin]
'Moorish looking; dark complexioned'.
(Morris, Morrell, Morel, Morice, Maurey, Morry, Morrie, Maury, Mo)

Maximilian [Latin]
'The greatest; the most excellent'. One without equal.
(Max, Maxey, Maxie, Maxim, Maxy, Maximilien)

Maxwell [Anglo-Saxon]
'Large spring'.
(Max, Maxie, Maxi)

Mayer [Latin]
'Greater'. The major character.
(Myer)

Mayfield [Anglo-Saxon]
'From the field of the warrior'.

Mayhew [French]
' Gift of God '. Another form of Matthew.

Maynard [Teutonic]
' Powerfully strong; brave '.
(Menard)

Mayo [Gaelic]
' From the plain of the yew trees '.

Mead [Anglo-Saxon]
' From the meadow '.

Medwin [Teutonic]
' Strong and powerful friend '.

Melbourne [Anglo-Saxon]
' From the mill stream '.
(Melburn, Melburne, Milbourn, Milbourne, Milburne, Milburn)

Meldon [Anglo-Saxon]
' From the mill on the hill '.

Melville [French]
' From the estate of the industrious '.
(Melvil, Mel)

Melvin See **Malvin**

Mendel [Semitic]
' Wisdom '.

Mercer [Anglo-Saxon]
' Merchant '.

Meredith [Welsh]
' Guardian from the sea '.
(Meredydd, Meridith, Merideth, Meredyth, Meridyth, Merry)

Merle [Latin]
' The blackbird; the black haired one '.

Merlin [Anglo-Saxon]
' The falcon '. The legendary wizard of King Arthur's court.
(Marlin, Marlen, Marlon, Marl, Merl)

Merrick See **Emery**

Merrill [French]
' Little famous one '.
(Merritt)

Merton [Anglo-Saxon]
' From the farm by the sea '.

Mervin See **Marvin**

Meyer [Teutonic]
' Steward '.

Michael [Hebrew]
' Like unto the Lord '.
(Micah, Mitchell, Michel, Mitch, Mich, Mike, Mickie, Micky)

Miles [Greek/Latin]
' The millstone ' (Greek) or ' The soldier ' (Latin).

Milford [Anglo-Saxon]
' From the mill ford '.
(Millford)

Millard [French]
' Strong and victorious '.

Miller [Anglo-Saxon]
' Grain grinder '.

Milo (Latin)
' The miller '.

Milton [Anglo-Saxon]
' From the mill town '.

Milward [Anglo-Saxon]
' The mill keeper '.

Miner [French/Latin]
' A miner ' (French); ' Young person ' (Latin).
(Minor)

Mischa See **Michael**

Mitchell See **Michael**

Modred [Anglo-Saxon]
' Brave counsellor '. One who advised honestly without fear of reprisal.

Monroe [Celtic]
' From the red swamp '.
(Munro, Monro, Munroe)

Montague [French]
' From the pointed mountain '.
(Monte, Monty, Montagu)

Montgomery [French]
' The mountain hunter '.
(Monte, Monty)

Moore [French]
' Dark complexioned; Moor '.
(More)

Moreland [Anglo-Saxon]
' From the moors '.

Morgan [Welsh]
'White sea '. The foam flecked waves.
(Morgen)

Morley [Anglo-Saxon]
' From the moor meadow '.

Morris See **Maurice**

Morrison [Anglo-Saxon]
' Maurice's son '.
(Morison)

Morse [Anglo-Saxon]
' Maurice's son '.

Mortimer [French]
' From the quiet water '.
(Mortemer, Mortermer, Morthermer)

Morton [Anglo-Saxon]
' From the farm on the moor '.

Morven [Gaelic]
' Blond giant '.
(Morfin)

Moses [Hebrew]
' Saved from the water '. The great prophet of Israel.
(Moise, Mose, Mosie, Moe, Moss)

Muir [Celtic]
' From the moor '.

Munroe See **Monroe**

Murdoch [Celtic]
' Prosperous from the sea '.
(Murdock, Murtagh)

Murphy [Gaelic]
' Sea warrior '.

Murray [Celtic]
' The mariner; sea fighter '

Myles See **Miles**

Myron [Greek]
' The fragrant oil '.
(Merrill)

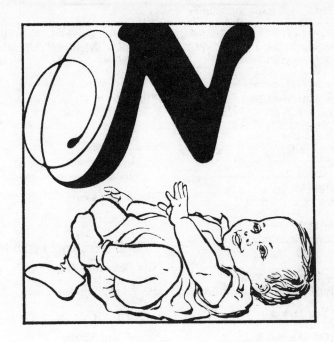

Girls

Nadine [French]
'Hope'.
(Nada, Nadia)

Naida [Latin]
'The water nymph'. From
the streams of Arcadia.
(Naiada)

Nairne [Gaelic]
'From the river'.

Nancy See Ann

Naomi [Hebrew]
'The pleasant one'.
*(Naoma, Noami, Nomi,
Nomie)*

Napea [Latin]
'Girl of the valley'.
(Napaea, Napia)

Nara [English]
'Nearest and dearest'. Also
dim. of Narda.

Narda [Latin]
'Fragrant perfume'. The
lingering essence.
(Nara)

Natalie [Latin]
'Born at Christmas tide'.
*(Natalia, Natala, Natale, Na-
tasha, Nathalie, Natica,*

Natika, Natacha, Natividad,
Nattie, Netta, Nettie, Netty,
Noel, Noelle Novella)

Nathania [Hebrew]
'Gift of God'.
(Natene, Nathene, Nathane)

Neale [Gaelic]
'The champion'. Fem. of
Neil.

Nebula [Latin]
'A cloud of mist'.

Neda [Slav]
'Born on Sunday'.
(Nedda)

Nelda [Anglo-Saxon]
'Born under the elder tree'.

Nell See **Helen**

Nellwyn [Greek]
'Bright friend and com-
panion'.

Neola [Greek]
'The young one'.

Neoma [Greek]
'The new moon'.

Nerima [Greek]
'From the sea'.
*(Nerissa, Nerine, Nerita,
Nerice)*

Netta See **Antonia, Henrietta,
Natalia**, etc.

Neva [Spanish]
'As white as the moon'.
(Nevada)

Neysa See **Agnes**

Nicole [Greek]
'The people's victory'.

(Nicola, Nichola, Nicholina,
Nicol, Nicolina, Nicoline,
Nikola, Nikki, Nickie,
Nicky)

Nila [Latin]
'From the Nile'.
(Nela)

Nina [Spanish]
'The daughter'.
(Nineta, Ninetta, Ninette)

Ninon See **Ann**

Nissa [Scandinavian]
'Friendly elf'. A fairy who
can be seen only by lovers.

Nita See **Ann, Jane**

Nixie [Teutonic]
'Water sprite'.
(Nissie, Nissy)

Noami See **Naomi**

Noelle See **Natalia**

Nokomis [American Indian]
'The grandmother'. From
the legend of Hiawatha.

Nola [Gaelic]
'Famous one'. See also
Olivia.

Noleta [Latin]
'Unwilling'.
(Nolita)

Nona [Latin]
'Ninth born'.

Nora See **Honora, Eleanor,
Helen**

Norberta [Teutonic]
'Bright heroine'.
*(Norberte, Norbertha, Nor-
berthe)*

Nordica [Teutonic]
' Girl from the North '.
(Nordika)

Norma [Latin]
' A pattern, or rule '. The template of the perfect girl.
(Normi, Normie)

Norna [Norse]
' Destiny '. The goddess of Fate.

Novia [Latin]
' The newcomer '.
(Nova)

Nuala [Gaelic]
' Fair shouldered one '.

Numidia [Latin]
' The traveller '.

Nydia [Latin]
' A refuge '.

Nyssa [Greek]
' Starting point '.

Nyx [Greek]
' White haired '.

Nairn [Celtic]
' Dweller by the alder tree '

Naldo See Reginald

Nathan [Hebrew]
' Gift of God '.
(Nathaniel, Nat, Nataniel, Nate, Nattie)

Neal [Gaelic]
' The champion '.
(Niall, Neil, Neill, Neall, Neale, Neel, Niels, Niles, Nils)

Ned See Edward/Edmund

Nelson [Celtic]
' Son of Neal '.

Nemo [Greek]
' From the glen '.

Nero [Latin]
' Dark complexioned, black haired '.

Nestor [Greek]
' Ancient wisdom '.

Neville [Latin]
' From the new town '
(Nevil, Nevile, Nev)

Nevin [Anglo-Saxon/Gaelic]
' The nephew ' (Anglo-Saxon) or ' Worshipper of Saints ' (Gaelic).
(Nevins, Niven, Nivens)

Newell [Anglo-Saxon]
' From the new hall '.
(Newall)

Newland [Anglo-Saxon]
' From the new lands '.
(Newlands)

Newlin [Celtic]
' Dweller by the new pool '.
(Newlyn)

Newman [Anglo-Saxon]
' The newcomer; the new arrival '.

Newton [Anglo-Saxon]
' From the new estate '.

Nial See Neal

Nicholas [Greek]
' Victorious people's army '. The leader of the people.
(Nicolas, Nichol, Nicholl, Niles, Nicol, Neacail, Nick. Nickie, Nicky, Nik, Nikki, Cole, Claus, Klaus, Colin, Colley)

Nicodemus [Greek]
' Conqueror for the people '.
(Nick, Nickie, Nicky, Nik, Nikki, Nikky)

Nigel [Latin]
' Black haired one '.

Niles See Nicholas/Neal

Nixon [Anglo-Saxon]
' Nicholas's son '.
(Nickson)

Noah [Hebrew]
' Rest, comfort and peace '.

Noble [Latin]
' Noble and famous '.
(Nobel, Nolan)

Noel [French]
' Born at Christmas '. A suitable name for a boy born on Christmas Day.

(Nowell, Newel, Newell, Natal, Natale)

Nolan See **Noble**

Noll See **Oliver**

Norbert [Teutonic]
'Brilliant sea hero'. The courageous commander of ships.

Norman [French]
'Man from the north; a Northman'. The venturesome and bold Viking from Scandinavia.
(Normand, Norris, Normie, Norm)

Norris See **Norman**

Northcliffe [Anglo-Saxon]
'Man from the north cliff'.
(Northcliff)

Northrop [Anglo-Saxon]
'From the northern farm'.
(Northrup, Nortrop, Nortrup)

Norton [Anglo-Saxon]
'From the north farm'.

Norville [French]
'From the north town'.
(Norvil, Norvel, Norvic)

Norvin [Anglo-Saxon]
'Friend from the north'.
(Norwyn, Norwin, Norvyn)

Norward [Anglo-Saxon]
'Guardian from the north'.

Norwell [Anglo-Saxon]
'From the north well'.

Norwood [Anglo-Saxon]
'From the north forest'.

Nowell See **Noel**

Nye See **Aneurin**

Girls

Obelia [Greek]
'A pointed pillar'.

Octavia [Latin]
'The eighth child'.
(Octavie, Ottavia, Ottavie, Tavia, Tavi, Tavie, Tavy)

Odelette [French]
'A small lyric'.
(Odelet)

Odelia [Teutonic]
'Prosperous one'.
(Odelie, Odella, Odelinda, Odilla, Odilia, Otha, Othilla, Ottilie)

Odessa [Greek]
'A long journey'.

Odette [French]
'Home lover'. One who makes a house into a home.

Ola [Scandinavia]
'Descendant'. The daughter of a chief.

Olga [Teutonic]
'Holy'. One who has been anointed in the service of God.
(Olva, Olivia, Olive, Elga, Livi, Livie, Livia, Livvi, Ollie)

Olinda [Latin]
'Fragrant herb'.

Olive [Latin]
'Symbol of peace'. The olive branch. Also der. of Olga.
(Olivia, Livia, Nollie, Nola, Olivette, Olva)

Olwyn [(Welsh]
(Olwen)

Olympia [Greek]
'Heavenly one'.
(Olympe, Olympie, Olimpie)

Ona See **Una**

Onawa [American Indian]
'Maiden who is wide awake'.

Oona, Oonagh See **Una**

Opal [Sanskrit]
'Precious jewel'.
(Opalina, Opaline)

Ophelia [Greek]
'Wise and immortal'.
(Ofelia, Ofilia, Phelia)

Ora [Latin]
'Golden one'.
(Orabel, Orabella, Orabelle)

Oralia See **Aurelia**

Ordelia [Teutonic]
'Elf's spear'.

Orea [Greek]
'Of the mountain'. The original maid of the mountains.

Orela [Latin]
'Divine pronouncement'. The oracle.

Orenda [American Indian]
'Magic power'.

Oriana [Latin]
'Golden one'.

Oriel See **Oralia**

Orna [Gaelic]
'Pale coloured'.

Orpah [Hebrew]
'A fawn'. From the Song of Solomon.

Ora See **Ursula**

Orva [Teutonic]
'Spear friend'.

Ottilie See **Odelia**

Ozora [Hebrew]
'Strength of the Lord'.

Oakes [Anglo-Saxon]
' Dweller by the oak tree '

Oakley [Anglo-Saxon]
' From the oak tree meadow '.
(Oakly, Okely, Okeley)

Obadiah [Hebrew]
' Servant of the Lord '. The
obedient one.

Obert [Teutonic]
' Wealthy and brilliant '.

Octavius [Latin]
' The eighth born '.
*(Octave, Octavian, Octavus,
Tavey)*

Odell [Teutonic]
' Wealthy one '.
(Odin, Odo)

Odolf [Teutonic]
' The wealthy wolf '.

Ogden [Anglo-Saxon]
' From the oak valley '.

Ogilvie [Celtic]
' From the high peak '.

Oglesby [Anglo-Saxon]
' Awe inspiring '.

Olaf [Scandinavian]
' Ancestral relic ' or ' Peaceful
reminder '.
(Olav, Olen, Amhlaoibh)

Olin See **Olaf**

Oliver [Latin]
' Symbol of peace '. The olive
branch.
*(Oliver, Ollie, Noll, Nollie,
Nolly)*

Olney [Anglo-Saxon]
' Olla's island '.

Omar [Arabic]
' The first son ' or ' Most high
follower of the Prophet '.

Onslow [Anglo-Saxon]
' Hill of the zealous one '.

Oram [Anglo-Saxon]
' From the enclosure by the
riverbank '.

Oran [Gaelic]
' Pale skinned man '.
*(Oren, Orin, Orran, Orren,
Orrin)*

Ordway [Anglo-Saxon]
' The spear fighter '.

Orestes [Greek]
' The mountain climber '.

Orford [Anglo-Saxon]
' Dweller at the cattle ford '.

Orion [Greek]
' The son of light '.

Orlan [Anglo-Saxon]
' From the pointed land '.

Orlando See **Roland**

Ormond [Teutonic]
' Spearman ' or ' Shipman '.
*(Orman, Ormand, Ormen,
Ormin)*

Oro [Spanish]
' Golden haired one '.

Orrick [Anglo-Saxon]
' Dweller by the ancient oak
tree '.

Orrin See **Oran**

Orson [Latin/Anglo-Saxon]
' Little bear ' (Latin) or ' Son of the spearman '

Orton [Anglo-Saxon]
' From the shore-farmstead '.

Orval [Anglo-Saxon]
' Spear mighty '.

Orville [French]
' From the golden town '.
(Orvil)

Orvin [Anglo-Saxon]
' Spear friend '.

Osbert [Anglo-Saxon]
' Divinely bright warrior '.
(Bert, Bertie, Berty, Oz, Ozzie)

Osborn [Anglo-Saxon]
' Divine warrior '.
(Osborne, Osburn, Osburne, Osbourn, Osbourne)

Oscar [Anglo-Saxon]
' Divine spearman '. 'A fighter for God '.
(Oskar, Oz, Ozzie, Os, Ossie)

Osgood [Scandinavian]
' The divine Goth '.

Osmar [Anglo-Saxon]
' Divinely glorious '.

Osmond [Anglo-Saxon]
' Divine protector '.

Osred [Anglo-Saxon]
' Divine counsellor '.

Oswald [Anglo-Saxon]
' Divinely powerful '.

Othman [Teutonic]
' The prosperous one '.

Otis [Greek]
' Keen of sight and hearing '.

Otto [Teutonic]
' Wealthy, prosperous man '.
(Otho)

Owen [Celtic]
' The young, well born warrior '.
(Owain, Evan)

Oxford [Anglo-Saxon]
' From the ford where oxen crossed '.

Oxton [Anglo-Saxon]

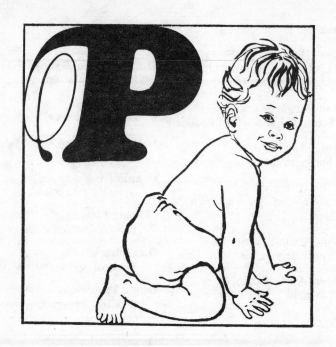

Girls

Paige [Anglo-Saxon]
 'Young child'.
 (Page)

Pallas [Greek]
 'Wisdom and knowledge'.
 Another name for the
 Goddess of Wisdom.

Paloma [Spanish]
 'The dove'. A gentle, tender
 girl.
 (Palometa, Palomita)

Pamela [Greek]
 'All sweetness and honey'. A
 loving person of great kind-
 ness.

*(Pamella, Pamelina, Pammie,
Pammy, Pam)*

Pandora [Greek]
 'Talented, gifted one'.

Pamphila [Greek]
 'All loving'. One who loves
 all humanity.

Pansy [Greek]
 'Fragrant, flowerlike'.

Panthea [Greek]
 'Of all the Gods'.
 (Panthia)

Parnella [French]
'Little rook'.
(Parnelle, Pernella, Pernelle)

Patience [Latin]
'Patient one'. A popular
'virtue' name.
(Pattie, Patty, Patienza)

Patricia [Latin]
'Well born maiden'. A girl
born to the noblest of
families.
*(Patrice, Patrizia, Pat, Patti,
Patty, Patsy)*

Paula [Latin]
'Little'. Fem. of Paul.
*(Paule, Paulette, Paulina,
Pauline, Paulita, Pauletta,
Pauli, Paulie)*

Peace [Latin]
'Tranquillity, calm'.

Pearl [Latin]
'Precious jewel'. One of un-
matched beauty. Also der. of
Margaret.
*(Pearle, Perle, Perl, Perlie,
Perline, Perlina, Pearlie)*

Peggy See **Margaret**

Pelagia [Greek]
'Mermaid'.

Penelope [Greek]
'The weaver'. The patient
wife of Ulysses who stitched
while he roamed.
(Pen, Penny)

Penthea [Greek]
'Fifth child'.
(Penta, Penthia)

Peony [Latin]
'The gift of healing'.

Pepita See **Josephine**

Perdita [Latin]
'The lost one'.

Perfecta [Spanish]
'The most perfect being'.

Pernella See **Parnella**

Persephone [Greek]
'Goddess of the under-
world'.

Persis [Latin]
'Woman from Persia'.

Petrina [Greek]
'Steadfast as a rock'. Fem.
of Peter.
*(Petra, Petronia, Petula,
Petronella, Petronelle, Petro-
nilla, Petronille, Pierette,
Pierrette, Perrine)*

Petunia [Indian]
'Reddish flower'.

Phedra [Greek]
'Bright one'. The daughter
of Minos of Crete.
(Phaidra, Phedre)

Philana [Greek]
'Friend of humanity'.
(Filana)

Philantha [Greek]
'Lover of flowers'. Child of
the blossoms.
(Philanthe, Filantha)

Philberta [Teutonic]
'Very brilliant'.
*(Philberthe, Philbertha, Fil-
berta, Filberte, Filbertha, Fil-
berthe)*

Philippa [Greek]
' Lover of horses '. Fem. of Philip.
(Phillippa, Phillipa, Pippa, Phillie, Filippa, Filipa)

Philomela [Greek]
' Lover of song '.

Philomena [Greek]
' Lover of the moon '. The nightingale.

Phoebe [Greek]
' Bright, shining sun '. Fem. of Phoebus (Apollo).
(Phebe)

Phoenix [Greek]
' The eagle '. The legendary bird who renewed its youth in its own ashes.
(Fenix)

Phyllis [Greek]
' A green bough '.
(Phyllida, Phillida, Phillis, Philis, Phylis, Fillida, Filida, Filis, Fillis)

Pierette See **Petrina**

Pilar [Spanish]
' A foundation or pillar '.

Piper [English]
' Player of the pipes '.

Placida [Latin]
' Peaceful one '.
(Placidia)

Platona [Greek]
' Broad shouldered '. Fem. of Plato. A woman of wisdom.

Polly See **Mary**

Pomona [Latin]
' Fruitful and fertile '.

Poppy [Latin]
' Red flower '.
(Poppaea)

Portia [Latin]
' An offering to God '.
(Porcia)

Poupée [French]
'Doll'

Presiley

Prima [Latin]
' First born '.

Primavera [Spanish]
' Child of the spring '.

Primrose [Latin]
' The first flower '. The harbinger of spring.
(Primula, Primmie, Rose, Rosa)

Priscilla [Latin]
' Of ancient lineage '. The descendant of princes.
(Prisilla, Pris, Prissie, Cilla)

Prospera [Latin]
' Favourable '.

Prudence [Latin]
' Cautious foresight '.
(Prudentia, Prud, Pruc, Prudie, Prudy)

Prunella [French]
' Plum coloured '.
(Prunelle)

Psyche [Greek]
   ' Of the soul or mind '. The
   true inner being.

Pyrena [Greek]
   ' Fiery one '. The warmth of
   the home.
   (Pyrenia)

Pythia [Greek]
   ' A prophet '. The oracle.
   (Pythea)

Paddy See **Patrick**

Padgett [French]
'The young attendant; a page.'
(Padget, Paget, Page)

Paine [Latin]
'The country rustic; a pagan'.
(Payne)

Palmer [Latin]
'The palm bearing pilgrim'.

Park [Anglo-Saxon]
'From the park'.
(Parke)

Parker [Anglo-Saxon]
'The park keeper'. One who guarded the park lands.

Parkin [Anglo-Saxon]
'Little Peter'.
(Perkin, Peterkin)

Parnell See **Peter**

Parr [Anglo-Saxon]
'Dweller by the cattle pen'.

Parrish [Anglo-Saxon]
'From the church parish'.
(Parish)

Parry [Celtic/French]
'Harry's son (Ap Harry)' or 'Protector' (French).

Pascal [Italian]
'Easter born'. The new born pascal lamb.

Patrick [Latin]
'The noble patrician'. One of noble birth and from a noble line.

(Patric, Padraic, Peyton, Padraig, Padruig, Patrice, Paddy, Pat, Patsy, Rick)

Patton [Anglo-Saxon]
'From the warrior's farm'.

Paul [Latin]
'Little'.
(Pablo, Paolo, Paley, Paulie, Pauley)

Paxton [Anglo-Saxon]
'From the warrior's estate'.

Payne See **Paine**

Payton [Anglo-Saxon]
'Dweller on the warrior's farm'.

Pedro See **Peter**

Pell [Anglo-Saxon]
'Scarf'.

Pelton [Anglo-Saxon]
'From the farm by the pool'.

Pembroke [Celtic]
'From the headland'.

Penley [Anglo-Saxon]
'From the enclosed meadow'.

Penn [Anglo-Saxon]
'Enclosure'.

Penrod [Teutonic]
'Famous commander'.

Pepin [Teutonic]
'The petitioner' or 'The persevered'.
(Peppin, Pepi, Peppi)

Percival [French]
'Valley piercer'.
(Parsefal, Parsifal, Perceval,

Percy, Perc, Perce, Purcell)

Perkin/Perrin See **Parkin**

Peregrine [Latin]
'The wanderer'.
(Perry)

Perry [Anglo-Saxon]
'From the pear tree'. Also
dim. of Peregrine.

Perth [Celtic]
'Thorn bush thicket'.

Peter [Latin]
'The stone; the rock'. The
first Pope.
*(Parnell, Pearce, Pedro,
Pernell, Perrin, Petrie, Pierce,
Pierre, Pietro, Pete, Peadar,
Pierrot, Pierro, Piero)*

Peverall [French]
'The piper'.
*(Peverell, Peverill, Peveral,
Peverel, Peveril)*

Peyton See **Payton**

Phelan [Gaelic]
'Brave as the wolf'.

Phelps [Anglo-Saxon]
'Son of Philip'.

Philip [Greek]
'Lover of horses'.
*(Philipp, Phillip, Phillipp,
Filip, Fillip, Phelps, Pilib,
Filib, Phil, Phillie, Philly)*

Phillips [Anglo-Saxon]
'Philip's son'.

*(Phelips, Phellips, Phellipps,
Philips, Phillipps, Felips,
Fellips)*

Philo [Greek]
'Friendly love'.

Phineas [Greek]
'Mouth of brass'.

Pickford [Anglo-Saxon]
'From the ford at the peak'.

Pickworth [Anglo-Saxon]
'From the estate of the
hewer'.

Pierce See **Peter**

Pitney [Anglo-Saxon]
'Persevering one's island'.

Pitt [Anglo-Saxon]
'From the hollow'.

Plato [Greek]
'The broad shouldered one'.
The great philosopher.

Platt [French]
'From the plateau'.

Pollock [Anglo-Saxon]
'Little Paul'.

Pomeroy [French]
'From the apple orchard'.

Porter [French]
'Gatekeeper'.

Powell [Celtic]
'Alert' or 'Son of Howell'
(Ap Howell)

Prentice [Anglo-Saxon]
'A learner or apprentice'.

Prescott [Anglo-Saxon]
'From the priest's house'.
(Prescot)

Preston [Anglo-Saxon]
'From the priest's farm'.

Prewitt [French]
'Little valiant warrior'.
(Prewit, Prewett, Prewet, Pruitt)

Price [Celtic]
'Son of a loving man'.

Primo [Latin]
'The first born son'.

Prior [Latin]
'The Father Superior, the Head of the Monastery'.
(Pryor)

Proctor [Latin]
'The administrator'.

Putnam [Anglo-Saxon]
'From the pit dweller's estate'.

Girls

Queena [Teutonic]
'The queen'. The supreme woman.
(Queenie)

Querida [Spanish]
'Beloved one'. A term of endearment.
(Cherida)

Quenby [Scandinavian]
'Womanly; the perfect wife'.

Quinta [Latin]
'The fifth child'.
(Quintina)

Quennel [French]
'Dweller by the little oak'.

Quentin [Latin]
'The fifth born'.
(Quinton, Quintin, Quent)

Quigley [Gaelic]
'Distaff'.

Quillan [Gaelic]
'Cub'.

Quillon [Latin]
'Sword'.

Quimby [Norse]
'From the woman's estate'.
(Quinby, Quemby, Quenby)

Quincy [French/Latin]
'From the fifth son's estate'.

Quinlan [Gaelic]
'The well formed one.' One with the body of an Adonis.

Quinn [Gaelic]
'Wise and intelligent'.

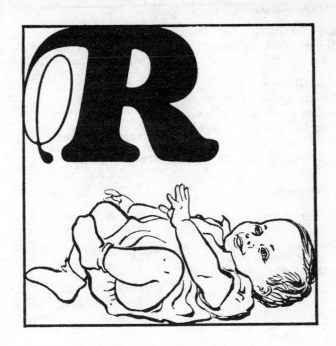

Girls

Rabi [Arabic]
'The harvest'.

Rachel [Hebrew]
'Innocent as a lamb'. One who suffers in silence.
(Rachele, Rachelle, Raquel, Rahel, Raoghnailt, Rochelle, Rae, Ray, Shelley)

Radella [Anglo-Saxon]
'Elf-like adviser'. A fairy-like creature whose advice is weighty.

Redinka [Slavic]
'Alive and joyful'.

Radmilla [Slavic]
'Worker for the people'.

Rae [Middle English]
'A doe deer'. Also dim. of Rachel.

Raina See **Regina**

Raissa [French]
'The believer'.
(Raisse)

Ramona [Teutonic]
'Wise protector'. Fem. of Raymond.
(Ramonda, Raymonde, Raymonda, Mona, Rama)

Rama [Sanskrit]
' Of royal birth; a queen '.
(Ranee, Rani)

Raphaela [Hebrew]
' Blessed healer '. One having
the God-given healing touch.
*(Rafaela, Rafaella, Rapha-
ella)*

Rasia See **Rose**

Ray See **Rachel**

Rebecca [Hebrew]
' The captivator '.
*(Rebeka, Rebekah, Rebekka,
Rebeca, Reba, Riva, Riba,
Beckie, Becky, Bekky)*

Regina [Latin]
' A queen; born to rule '.
*(Regan, Regine, Raina,
Reine, Raine, Rayna, Reina,
Rioghnach, Rina, Gina,*

Renata [Latin]
' Born again '. The spirit of
reincarnation.
*(Rene, Renee, Rennie, Ren-
ate)*

Rene See **Irene, Renata**

Renita [Latin]
' A rebel '.

Reseda [Latin]
' Mignonette flower '.

Reva [Latin]
' Strength regained '.

Rexana [Latin]
' Regally graceful '. One
whose bearing is regal.
(Rexanna)

Rhea [Greek]
' Mother ' or ' Poppy '. The
mother of the Grecian Gods.
(Rea)

Rheta [Greek]
' An orator '.

Rhiannon [Welsh]

Rhoda [Greek]
' Garland of roses; girl from
Rhodes '. *(Rhodia)*

Rhodanthe [Greek]
' The rose of roses '.

Ria [Spanish]
' The river '.

Ricarda [Teutonic]
' Powerful ruler '. Fem. of
Richard. *(Richarda, Ric-
harde, Rickie, Ricky,
Dickie, Dicky)*

Ricadonna [Italian]
' Ruling lady '. One who rules
in her own right or on behalf
of her son.

Rilla [Teutonic]
' A stream or brook '.
(Rille, Rillette)

Rita See **Margaret**

Riva [French]
' Riverbank '.

Roanna [Latin]
' Sweet and gracious '.
(Rohanna, Rohanne)

Roberta [Anglo-Saxon]
' Of shining fame '. Fem. of
Robert.
*(Robina, Roberta, Robinia,
Robinette, Robertha, Rober-*

the, *Ruberta*, *Ruperta*, *Bob-ette*, *Bobina*, *Bobbie*, *Bobby*, *Bertie)*

Rochelle [French]
' From the small rock '.
(Rochalla, Rochalle, Roch-ella, Rochette)

Roderica [Teutonic]
' Famous ruler'. Fem. of Roderick.
(Rodericka, Rica, Roddie, Roddy, Rickie)

Rohana [Hindu]
' Sandalwood; sweet incense '.
(Rohanna, Rohane)

Rohesia See **Rose**

Rolanda [Teutonic]
' From the famed land '. Fem. of Roland.
(Rolande, Orlanda, Orlande, Ro, Rola)

Roma [Latin]
' Woman of Rome '.

Romilda [Teutonic]
' Glorious warrior maiden '.
(Romilde, Romhilda, Rom-hilde)

Romola [Latin]
' Lady of Rome '.
(Romella, Romelle)

Ronalda [Teutonic]
' All powerful'. Fem. of Ronald.
(Ronalde, Ronnie, Ronny)

Rosabel [Latin]
' Beautiful rose '.
(Rosabella, Rosabelle)

Rosalie See **Rose**

Rosalind [Latin]
' Fair and beautiful rose '.
(Rosalinda, Rosaline, Rosa-lynd, Rosaline, Roseline, Roselyn, Rosalyn, Roslyn, Ros, Roz, Rozalind, Roza-line, Rozeline)

Rosamond [French]
' Rose of the world '.
(Rosemond, Rosemund, Ros-amund, Rosamunda, Rosa-monda, Rosmunda, Rose-monde, Rozamond)

Rosanna [English]
' Graceful rose '.
(Rosanne)

Rose [Greek]
' The rose '. The most beauti-ful of flowers '.
(Rosa, Rosie, Rosalie, Rosa-lia, Rosella, Rohesia, Roselle, Rosetta, Rosette, Rosina, Rasia, Rosia, Rozello, Rhoda, Rhodia, Rosalee, Rosaleen, Rosena, Rosene, Rosel, Roz-ina, Rosella, Rosy)

Rosemary [Latin]
' Dew of the sea '.
(Rosemarie)

Rosetta See **Rose**

Roux See **Laroux**

Rowena [Anglo-Saxon]
' Friend with white hair '.
(Rowenna)

Roxana [Persian]
' Brilliant dawn '.
(Roxane, Roxanna, Roxanne, Roxine, Roxina, Rox, Roxie, Roxy)

Royale [French]
'Regal being'. Fem. of Roy.

Ruby [Latin]
'Precious red jewel'.
(Rubetta, Rubette, Rubia, Rubina, Rubie)

Rudelle [Teutonic]
'Famous person'.
(Rudella)

Ruella [Combination
                    Ruth/Ella]

Rufina [Latin]
'Red-haired one'.

Rula [Latin]
'A sovereign'. One who rules by right.

Ruth [Hebrew]
'Compassionate and beautiful'.
(Ruthie)

Rad [Anglo-Saxon]
'Counsellor; adviser'. Also dim. of Radcliffe.

Radbert [Teutonic]
'Brilliant counsellor'.

Radborne [Anglo-Saxon]
'From the red stream'.
(Radbourne, Redbourne, Radbourn, Redbourn)

Radcliffe [Anglo-Saxon]
'From the red cliff'.
(Radcliff, Redcliff, Redcliffe)

Radford [Anglo-Saxon]
'From the red ford'.
(Redford, Radvers, Redvers)

Radley [Anglo-Saxon]
'From the red meadow'.
(Radleigh)

Radnor [Anglo-Saxon]
'From the red shore'.

Radolf [Anglo-Saxon]
'Wolf counsellor'. Wolf is used in the sense 'brave man'.

Rafael See **Raphael**

Rafferty [Gaelic]
'Prosperous and rich'.

Raleigh [Anglo-Saxon]
'Dweller in the meadow of the roe deer'.
(Ralegh, Rawley, Rawleigh)

Ralph [Anglo-Saxon]
'Counsel wolf'.
(Ralf, Raff, Rolf, Rolph, Raoul)

Ralston [Anglo-Saxon]
'Dweller on Ralph's farm'.

Rambert [Teutonic]
'Brilliant and mighty'.

Ramon See **Raymond**

Ramsden [Anglo-Saxon]
'Ram's valley'.

Ramsey [Anglo-Saxon]
'From Ram's island' or 'From the raven's island'.

Randal [Old English]
'Shield wolf'
(Randall, Rand, Randolph, Randolf, Ranulf)

Ranger [French]
'Keeper of the forest'. The gamekeeper who looked after the trees and the wildlife.

Rankin [Anglo-Saxon]
'Little shield'.

Ransford [Anglo-Saxon]
'From the raven's ford'.

Ransley [Anglo-Saxon]
'From the raven's meadow'.

Ransom [Anglo-Saxon]
'Shield warrior's son'.

Raoul See **Ralph**

Raphael [Hebrew]
'Healed by God'.
(Rafael, Rafaello, Raffaello Raff)

Rawlins [French]
'Son of the wolf counsellor'.

Rawson [Anglo-Saxon]
' Son of the little wolf '

Ray [French]
' The sovereign '. Also dim. of Raymond.

Raymond [Teutonic]
' Wise protection '.
(Raymon, Raimond, Reamonn, Raymund, Ray)

Raynor [Scandinavian]
' Mighty army '.
(Rainer, Rainier)

Reade [Anglo-Saxon]
' The red headed one '.
(Read, Reed, Reede)·

Reading [Anglo-Saxon]
' Son of the red haired one '.
(Redding)

Redford See **Radford**

Redley See **Radley**

Redman [Anglo-Saxon]
' Counsellor; advice giver '.

Redmond [Anglo-Saxon]
' Counsellor, protector, advisor '.
(Radmund, Redmund)

Redwald [Anglo-Saxon]
' Mighty counsellor '.

Reece [Celtic]
' The ardent one '. One who loves living.

Reed/Reid See **Reade**

Reeve [Anglo-Saxon]
' The steward '. One who looked after a great lord's affairs.

Regan [Gaelic]
' Royalty, a king '.
(Reagan, Reagen, Regen)

Reginald [Teutonic]
' Mighty and powerful ruler '.
(Raynold, Reinhold, Reynold, Ronald, Reg, Reggie, Reggy, Ron, Ronnie, Ronny)

Remington [Anglo-Saxon]
' From the farm where the blackbirds sing '.

Remus [Latin]
' Fast rower '. A speedy oarsman.

Renault See **Reginald**

Rene See **Reginald**

Renfred [Anglo-Saxon]
' Mighty and peaceful '. A peaceful warrior who could fight when necessary.

Renfrew [Celtic]
' From the still river '.

Renny [Gaelic]
' Little mighty and powerful '. Also der. of Rene.

Renshaw [Anglo-Saxon]
' From the forest of the ravens '.

Renton [Anglo-Saxon]
' From the farm of the roe buck '.

Reuben [Hebrew]
' Behold a son '.
(Ruben, Rube, Rubey, Ruby)

Rex [Latin]
' The king '. The all powerful monarch.
(Rey, Roy)

Rexford [Anglo-Saxon]
' From the king's ford '.

Reynard (Teutonic)
' Mighty courage ' or ' The fox '.
(Rehard, Rennard, Raynard, Reinhard, Renaud)

Reynold See **Reginald**

Rhodes [Greek]
' The place of roses '.

Rich See **Richard**

Richard [Teutonic]
' Wealthy, powerful one '.
(Ricard, Richerd, Rickert, Riocard, Rick, Rickie, Ricky, Rich, Ritch, Ritchie, Dick, Dickie, Dicky, Dickon, Diccon)

Richmond [Anglo-Saxon]
' Powerful protector '.
(Richman)

Ricker [Teutonic]
' Powerful army '.

Rickward [Anglo-Saxon]
' Powerful guardian '.
(Rickwood)

Riddock [Gaelic]
' From the barren field '.

Rider [Anglo-Saxon]
' Knight; horse-rider '.
(Ryder)

Ridge [Anglo-Saxon]
' From the ridge '

Ridgeway [Anglo-Saxon]
' From the ridge road '.

Ridgley [Anglo-Saxon]
' From the ridge meadow '.

Ridley See **Radley**

Ridpath [Anglo-Saxon]
' From the red path '.
(Redpath)

Rigby [Anglo-Saxon]
' Valley of the ruler '.

Rigg [Anglo-Saxon]
' From the ridge '.

Riley [Gaelic]
' Valiant and warlike '.
(Reilly, Ryley)

Ring [Anglo-Saxon]
' A ring '.

Riordan [Gaelic]
' Royal bard '
(Reardon, Rearden)

Ripley [Anglo-Saxon]
' From the valley of the echo '.

Risley [Anglo-Saxon]
' From the brushwood meadow '.

Riston [Anglo-Saxon]
' From the brushwood farm '.

Ritchie See **Richard**

Ritter [Teutonic]
' A knight '.

Roald [Teutonic]
' Famous ruler '.

Roan [Anglo-Saxon]
' From the rowan tree '.
(Rowan)

Roarke [Gaelic]
' Famous ruler '.
(Rorke, Rourke, Ruark)

141

Robert [Teutonic]
'Bright, shining fame'. A man of brilliant reputation.
(Roberto, Robin, Rupert, Ruprecht, Rob, Robbie, Robby, Rab, Rabbie, Rabby, Bob, Bobbie, Bobby)

Robinson [Anglo-Saxon]
'Son of Robert'.

Rochester [Anglo-Saxon]
'Camp on the rocks'.

Rock [Anglo-Saxon]
'From the rock'.
(Roc, Rocky)

Rockley [Anglo-Saxon]
'From the rocky meadow'.
(Rockly)

Rockwell [Anglo-Saxon]
'From the rocky well'.

Rodd See **Roderick**

Roden [Anglo-Saxon]
'From the valley of the reeds'.

Roderick [Teutonic]
'Famous, wealthy ruler'.
(Rodrick, Rodric, Roderic, Broderic, Broderick, Brodrick, Rod, Roddie, Roddy, Rick, Rickie, Ricky, Rory)

Rodger See **Roger**

Rodman [Teutonic]
'Famous hero'.
(Rodmond Rodmund)

Rodney [Teutonic]
'Famous and renowned'.
(Rod, Roddie, Roddy, Rodi)

Rodolph See **Rudolph**

Rodwell [Anglo-Saxon]
'From the Christian's well'.

Roe [Anglo-Saxon]
'Roe deer'.

Rogan [Gaelic]
'The red haired one'.

Roger [Teutonic]
'Famous spearman; renowned warrior'.
(Rodger, Rodge, Rog)

Roland [Teutonic]
'From the famed land'.
(Rollo, Rowe, Orlando, Rowland, Rollin, Roley, Rodhlann)

Rolf See **Ralph, Randolph, Rudolph**

Rollo See **Roland, Rudolph**

Rolt [Teutonic]
'Power and fame'.

Romeo [Latin]
'Man from Rome'.

Romney [Celtic]
'Curving river'.

Ronald See **Reginald**

Ronan [Gaelic]
'Little seal'.

Ronson [Anglo-Saxon]
'Son of Ronald'.

Rooney [Gaelic]
'The red one'. One with a ruddy complexion.
(Ruan, Rowney)

Roper [Anglo-Saxon]
'Rope maker'.

142

Rorke See **Roarke**

Rory [Gaelic]
'Red king'. Also der. of
Roderick. *(Ruaidhri/Irish,
Ruairidh/Scottish,
Rorie, Rorry)*

Roscoe [Scandinavian]
'From the deer forest'.
(Rosco, Ros, Roz)

Roslin [French]
'Small, red haired one'.
(Roslyn, Rosselin, Rosslyn)

Ross [Celtic]
'From the peninsula'. Alternatively, 'Horse' (Teutonic).

Roswald [Teutonic]
'Mighty steed'.
(Roswall, Roswell)

Rothwell [Norse]
'From the red well'.

Rourke See **Roarke**

Rover [Anglo-Saxon]
'A wanderer'.

Rowan [Gaelic]
'Red haired'.
(Rowen, Rowe)

Rowell [Anglo-Saxon]
'From the deer well'.

Rowland See **Roland**

Rowley [Anglo-Saxon]
'From the rough meadow'.

Rowsan [Anglo-Saxon]
'Rowan's son'. Son of a red
haired man.

Roxbury [Anglo-Saxon]
'From the fortress of the rock.'

Roy [Celtic]
'Red haired' or 'The king'.
(See Rex.)

Royal [French]
'Regal one'.

Royce [Anglo-Saxon]
'Son of the king'.

Royd [Norse]
'From the forest clearing'.

Roydon [Anglo-Saxon]
'Dweller on the rye hill'.

Ruben See **Reuben**

Ruck [Anglo-Saxon]
'The rock'. One with black
hair.

Rudd [Anglo-Saxon]
'Ruddy complexion'.

Rudolph [Teutonic]
'Famous wolf'.
*(Rudolf, Rodolf, Rolfe,
Rollo, Rolph, Rudy, Dolf,
Dolph)*

Rudyard [Anglo-Saxon]
'From the red enclosure'.

Ruff [French]
'The red haired one'.

Rufford [Anglo-Saxon]
'From the rough ford'.

Rufus [Latin]
'Red haired'.
*(Rufe, Ruff, Griffin, Griffith,
Griff)*

Rugby [Anglo-Saxon]
'From the rook estate'.

Rule [Latin]
'The ruler'.
(Ruelle)

Rumford [Anglo-Saxon]
'From the wide ford'.
(Romford)

Rupert See **Robert**

Rurik See **Roderick**

Rush [French]
'Red haired'.

Rushford [Anglo-Saxon]
'From the rush ford'.

Ruskin [Teutonic]
'Small red haired one'.

Rust [Anglo-Saxon]
'Red haired'.
(Russet, Rusty)

Russell [Anglo-Saxon]
'Red as a fox'.
(Rus, Russ, Rusty, Russel)

Rutherford [Anglo-Saxon]
'From the cattle ford'.

Rutland [Norse]
'From the stump land'.

Rutledge [Anglo-Saxon]
'From the red pool'.
(Routledge)

Rutley [Anglo-Saxon]
'From the stump meadow'.

Ryan [Gaelic]
'Small king'.

Rycroft [Anglo-Saxon]
'From the rye field'.

Ryder See **Rider**

Rye [French]
'From the riverbank'.

Rylan [Anglo-Saxon]
'From the rye land'.
(Ryland)

Ryle [Anglo-Saxon]
'From the rye hill'.

Ryley See **Riley**

Ryman [Anglo-Saxon]
'The rye-seller'.

Ryton [Anglo-Saxon]
'From the rye farm'.

Girls

Saba [Greek]
'Woman of Sheba'.

Sabina [Latin]
'Woman of Sabine'.
(Sabine, Savina, Bina, Saidhbhain)

Sabra [Hebrew]
'The restful one'.

Sabrina [Latin]
'A princess'.
(Brina, Sabrine)

Sacha [Greek]
'Helpmate'. *(Sasha)*

Sadie See **Sarah**

Sadira [Persian]
'The lotus eater'.

Salina [Greek]
'From the salty place'.

Sally See **Sarah**

Salome [Hebrew]
'Peace'. 'Shalom' the traditional Hebrew greeting—Peace.
(Saloma, Salomi)

Salvia [Latin]
'Sage herb'.
(Salvina)

Samantha [Aramaic]
' A listener '.

Samara [Hebrew]
' Watchful, cautious; guarded by God '.

Samuela [Hebrew]
' His name is God '. Fem. of Samuel.
(Samella, Samelle, Samuella, Samuelle)

Sancia [Latin]
' Sacred '.
(Sancha, Sanchia)

Sandra See **Alexandra**

Sapphira [Greek]
' Eyes of sapphire colour '.

Sarah [Hebrew]
' Princess '. One of royal status.
(Sara, Sari, Sarene, Sarine, Sarette, Sadella, Sadie, Sorcha, Salaidh, Sadye, Sal, Sallie, Sally, Sharie, Sarita, Zara, Zarah, Zaria)

Savanna [Spanish]
' An open plain '.

Savina See **Sabina**

Saxona [Teutonic]
' A sword bearer '.

Scarlett [Middle English]
' Scarlet coloured '.
(Scarlet, Scarletta)

Sebastiane [Latin]
' Revered one '.
(Sebastiana, Sebastianne, Sebastianna, Sebastienna, Sebastienne)

Secunda [Latin]
' Second born '.

Selena [Greek]
' The Moon '.
(Selina Selene, Selinda, Salene, Sela, Selie, Sena, Selia, Celene, Celina, Celinda, Celie, Lena)

Selma [Celtic]
' The fair '. Also der. of Anselma.

Semele [Latin]
' The single one '.
(Semelia)

Semira [Hebrew]
' Height of the heavens '.

Septima [Latin]
' Seventh born '.

Seraphina [Hebrew]
' The ardent believer '. One with a burning faith '.
(Serafina, Seraphine, Serafine, Sera)

Serena [Latin]
' Bright tranquil one '.

Serilda [Teutonic]
' Armoured battle maid '.
(Serilde, Serhilda, Serhilde)

Sharleen See **Charlotte/
Caroline**

Sharon [Hebrew]
' A princess of exotic beauty '.
(Sherry, Shari, Sharri, Sharry)

Sheba See **Saba**

Sheila [Celtic]
'Musical'. Var. of Cecilia.
(Sheela, Sheelah, Sheilah, Selia)

Shelley [English]
'From the edge of the meadow'.

Sheena [Gaelic]
Another var. of Jane

Sherry See **Charlotte, Sharon**

Sherri See **Cherie**

Sheryl See **Charlotte, Shirley**

Shirley [Anglo-Saxon]
'From the white meadow'.
(Shirlee, Shirlie, Shirleen, Shirlene, Sheryl, Sherry, Sheri)

Sibyl See **Sybil**

Sidney/Sidonia See **Sydney**

Sidra [Latin]
'Glittering lady of the stars'.
(Sidria)

Sigfreda [Teutonic]
'Victorious and peaceful'.
(Sigfrieda, Sigfriede)

Signa [Latin]
'Signed on the heart'.

Sigrid [Norse]
'Victorious counsellor'.
(Sigrath, Sigrud, Sigurd)

Simone [Hebrew]
'Heard by the Lord'. Fem. of Simon/Simeon.
(Simona, Simonette, Simonetta)

Sinead [Welsh] See **Jane**

Siobhan [Irish] See **Jane**

Sirena [Greek]
'Sweet singing mermaid'. Originally from the sirens who lured men to their deaths. Used sometimes during World War II for babies born during an air raid.
(Sirene, Sireen)

Siriol [Welsh]

Solita [Latin]
'Solitary one'.

Solvig [Teutonic]
'Victorious battle maid'.

Sonia See **Sophia**

Sophia [Greek]
'Wisdom'.
(Sophie, Sophy, Sofia, Sonia, Sonja, Sonya, Sofie, Sadhbh, Sadhbha, Beathag)

Sophronia [Greek]
'Sensible one'.

Sorcha [Gaelic]
'Bright one'.

Spring [English]
'Joyous season'.

Stacy/Stacia See **Anastasia/ Eustacia**

Starr [English]
'A star'.
(Star)

Stella See **Estelle**

Stephanie [Greek]
'A crown; garland'. Fem. of Stephen.

(Stephania, Stephena, Stevana, Stevania, Stevena, Stevenia, Stephenie, Stephenia, Stephena, Stefa, Stepha, Steffie, Stevie)

Storm [Anglo-Saxon]
'A tempest'. One of turbulent nature.

Sunny [Anglo-Saxon]
'Bright and cheerful'. The brightness of the sun after the storm.

Susan [Hebrew]
'Graceful lily'.
(Susana, Susanna, Susanne, Susannah, Suzanna, Suzanne, Suzette, Susette, Suzetta, Sue, Susi, Susie, Susy, Suzie, Suzy, Suki, Sukey, Suky, Zsa-Zsa)

Sybil [Greek]
'Prophetess'. The female soothsayer of ancient Greece.
(Sibyl, Sibil, Sibel, Sibell,
Sybyl, Sibilla, Sibella, Sybella, Sibille, Sibylle, Sybille, Sib, Sibie, Sibbie, Sibby)

Sydel [Hebrew]
'That enchantress'.
(Sydelle)

Sydney [French/Hebrew]
'From St. Denis' (French); 'The enticer' (Hebrew). Fem. of Sidney.
(Sidney, Sidonia, Sidonie, Sid, Syd)

Sylvia [Latin]
'From the forest'.
(Silvia, Silva, Sylva, Silvana, Slyvana, Zilvia, Zilva, Sil, Syl, Silvie)

Syna [Greek]
'Together'.
(Syne)

Saber [French]
'A sword'.

Sabin [Latin]
'Man from the Sabines'.

Safford [Anglo-Saxon]
'From the willow ford'.

Salton [Anglo-Saxon]
'From the willow farm'.

Salvador [Latin]
'The saviour'.
(Salvadore, Salvator, Salvatore)

Sampson [Hebrew]
'Sun's man'.
(Samson, Simpson, Simson, Sam, Sammy, Sim)

Samuel [Hebrew]
'His name is God'.
(Sam, Sammie, Sammy)

Sanborn [Anglo-Saxon]
'From the sandy brook'.
(Samborn)

Sancho [Spanish]
'Sincere and truthful'.

Sanders [Anglo-Saxon]
'Son of Alexander'.
(Sanderson, Saunderson, Saunders, Sandie, Sandy)

Sanford [Anglo-Saxon]
'From the sandy ford'.

Sansom See **Sampson**

Santo [Italian]
'Saint like'.

Santon [Anglo-Saxon]
'From the sandy farm'.

Sargent [Latin]
'A military attendant'.
(Sergeant, Sergent, Sarge, Sargie)

Saul [Hebrew]
'Called by God'.

Saville [French]
'The willow estate'.
(Savile)

Sawyer [Anglo-Saxon]
'A sawer of wood'.

Saxon [Anglo-Saxon]
'People of the swords'.
(Saxe)

Sayer [Celtic]
'Carpenter'.
(Sayre, Sayers, Sayres)

Scanlon [Gaelic]
'A snarer of hearts'.

Schuyler [Dutch]
'A scholar; a wise man' or 'To shield'.

Scott [Latin/Celtic]
'From Scotland' (Latin) or 'Tattoed warrior' (Celtic).
(Scot, Scottie, Scotty)

Scoville [French]
'From the Scottish estate'.

Scully [Gaelic]
'Town crier'. The bringer of news in the days before mass media.

Seabert [Anglo-Saxon]
'Sea glorious'.
(Seabright, Sebert)

Seabrook [Anglo-Saxon]
'From a brook by the sea'.
(Sebrook)

Seamus See **James**

Sean See **John**

Searle [Teutonic]
' Armed warrior '.
(Searl)

Seaton [French]
' From Say's farm '.
(Seton, Seeton, Seetin)

Sebastian [Latin]
' Reverenced one '. An august
person.
(Sebastien, Seb)

Sedgley [Anglo-Saxon]
' From the swordsman's
meadow '.
(Sedgeley)

Sedgwick [Anglo-Saxon]
' From the sword grass
place '.
(Sedgewick)

Seeley [Anglo-Saxon]
' Happy and blessed '.
(Seely, Sealey)

Seger [Anglo-Saxon]
' Sea warrior '.
(Seager, Segar)

Selby [Teutonic]
' From the manor farm '.

Selden [Anglo-Saxon]
' From the valley of the
willow tree '.

Selig [Teutonic]
' Blessed happy one '.

Selwyn [Teutonic]
' Friend at the manor house '.
(Selwin)

Senior [French]
' Lord of the manor '.
(Seigneur)

Sennett [French]
' Old and wise '. The all
knowing seer.

Septimus [Latin]
' Seventh born son '.

Serle [Teutonic]
' Bearer of arms and
weapons '.

Serge/Sergeant See **Sargeant**

Seth [Hebrew]
' The appointed by God '.

Seton [Anglo-Saxon]
' From the farm by the sea '.

Seumas [Gaelic] See **James**

Severn [Anglo-Saxon]
' The boundary '.

Seward [Anglo-Saxon]
' The sea defender '.

Sewell [Anglo-Saxon]
' Sea powerful '.
(Sewald, Sewall, Siwald)

Sexton [Anglo-Saxon]
' Sacristan '. A church official.

Sextus [Latin]
' Sixth born son '.

Seymour [**French/Anglo-Saxon**]
' From St. Maur ' (French) or
' From the sea moor '
(Anglo-Saxon).

Shadwell [Anglo-Saxon]
From the well in the
arbour '.

Shamus See **James**

Shanahan [Gaelic]
'The wise one'.

Shandy [Anglo-Saxon]
'Little boisterous one'.

Shane See **John**

Shanley [Gaelic]
'The venerable hero'.

Shannon [Gaelic]
'Old wise one'.

Shattuck [Anglo-Saxon]
'Little shad-fish'.

Shaw [Anglo-Saxon]
'From the grove'.

Shea [Gaelic]
'Stately, courteous, and inventive person'. A man of many parts.
(Shay)

Sheehan [Gaelic]
'Peaceful one'.

Sheffield [Anglo-Saxon]
'From the crooked field'.

Shelby [Anglo-Saxon]
'From the estate on the cliff edge'.

Sheldon [Anglo-Saxon]
'From the hill ledge'.

Shelley [Anglo-Saxon]
'From the meadow on the hill ledge'.

Shelton [Anglo-Saxon]
'From the farm on the hill ledge'.

Shepard [Anglo-Saxon]
'The sheep tender; the shepherd'.

(Shepherd, Sheppard, Shepperd, Shep, Shepp, Sheppy)

Shepley [Anglo-Saxon]
'From the sheep meadow'.

Sherborne [Anglo-Saxon]
'From the clear stream'.
(Sherbourn, Sherbourne, Sherburne, Sherburn)

Sheridan [Gaelic]
'Wild savage'.

Sherlock [Anglo-Saxon]
'White haired man'.

Sherman [Anglo-Saxon]
'Wool shearer; sheep shearer'.

Sherwin [Anglo-Saxon]
'Loyal friend' or 'Swift footed'.

Sherwood [Anglo-Saxon]
'Bright forest'.

Shipley [Anglo-Saxon]
'From the sheep meadow'.

Shipton [Anglo-Saxon]
'From the sheep farm'.

Sholto [Gaelic]
'The wild duck'.

Sian See **John**

Siddell [Anglo-Saxon]
'From a wide valley'.

Sidney [French]
'A follower of St. Denis' or 'Man from Sidon'.
(Sid, Syd, Sydney)

Sigfrid [Teutonic]
'Peace after victory'.
(Sigfried, Siegfrid, Siegfried)

Sigmund [Teutonic]
' Victorious protector '.
(Sigismund, Sigismond, Sigmond)

Sigurd [Scandinavian]
' Victorious guardian '.
(Sigerd)

Sigwald [Teutonic]
' Victorious ruler '.

Silas [Latin]
' From the forest '.
(Silvan, Silvanus, Silvester, Sylvan, Sylvester, Si)

Simon [Hebrew]
' One who hears '.
(Simeon, Siomonn, Sim)

Sinclair [French]
' From St. Clair ' or ' Shining light '.
(St. Clair)

Skeets [Anglo-Saxon]
' The swift '.
(Skeat, Skeet, Skeeter)

Skelly [Gaelic]
' Historian '.

Skelton [Anglo-Saxon]
' From the farm on the hill ledge '.

Skerry [Scandinavian]
' From the rocky island '.

Skip [Scandinavian]
' Owner of the ship '.
(Skipp, Skippy)

Skipton [Anglo-Saxon]
' From the sheep farm '.

Slade [Anglo-Saxon]
' Valley dweller '.

Slevin [Gaelic]
' The mountain climber '.
(Slaven, Slavin Sleven)

Sloan [Gaelic]
' Warrior '.
(Sloane)

Smedley [Anglo-Saxon]
' From the flat meadow '.
(Smedly)

Smith [Anglo-Saxon]
' The blacksmith '.

Snowden [Anglo-Saxon]
' From the snowy hill '. Man from the snowcapped mountains.

Sol [Latin]
' The sun '. Also dim. of Solomon.

Solomon [Hebrew]
' Wise and peaceful '. The wisdom of Solomon.
(Solamon, Soloman, Salomon, Sol, Sollie, Solly)

Solon [Greek]
' Wise man '. Greek form of Solomon.

Somerset [Anglo-Saxon]
' From the summer place '. The place where the wanderers rested for the summer.

Somerton [Anglo-Saxon]
' From the summer farm '.

Somerville [Anglo-Saxon]
' From the summer estate '.
(Sommerville)

Sorrel [French]
' With brownish hair '.

Southwell [Anglo-Saxon]
'From the south well'.

Spalding [Anglo-Saxon]
'From the split meadow'.
(Spaulding)

Spangler [Teutonic]
'The tinsmith'.

Spark [Anglo-Saxon]
'Gay gallant'. The man about town.

Speed [Anglo-Saxon]
'Success, prosperity'.

Spencer [French]
'Shopkeeper; dispenser of provisions'.
(Spenser, Spence)

Sproule [Anglo-Saxon]
'Energetic, active person'.
(Sprowle)

Squire [Anglo-Saxon]
'Knight's shield bearer'.

Stacey [Latin]
'Prosperous and stable'.
(Stacy)

Stafford [Anglo-Saxon]
'From the ford by the landing place'.

Stamford [Anglo-Saxon]
'From the stony crossing'.
(Stanford)

Stanbury [Anglo-Saxon]
'From a stone fortress'.
(Stanberry)

Stancliffe [Anglo-Saxon]
'From the rocky cliff'.

(Stancliff, Standcliff, Standcliffe)

Standish [Anglo-Saxon]
'From the stony park'.

Stanfield [Anglo-Saxon]
'From the stony field'.

Stanford See **Stamford**

Stanhope [Anglo-Saxon]
'From the stony hollow'.

Stanislaus [Slavic]
'Stand of glory'.
(Stanislas, Stanislav, Aineislis, Stan)

Stanley [Slavic/Anglo-Saxon]
'Pride of the camp' (Slavic) or 'From the stony meadow' (Anglo-Saxon).
(Stanley, Stanleigh, Stanly, Stan)

Stanton [Anglo-Saxon]
'From the rocky lake'.

Stanton [Anglo-Saxon]
'From the stony farm'.

Stanway [Anglo-Saxon]
'From the stony road'.

Stanwick [Anglo-Saxon]
'From the stony village'.

Stanwood [Anglo-Saxon]
'From the stony forest'.

Starling [Anglo-Saxon]
'The starling'.

Starr [Anglo-Saxon]
'A star'.

Stedman [Anglo-Saxon]
'Farm owner'. One who owns the land he tills.

Stein [Teutonic]
' The stone '.

Stephen [Greek]
' The crowned one '. A man who wears the victor's laurel wreath.
(Steven, Stephenson, Stevenson, Stefan, Steffen, Steve, Stevie)

Sterling [Teutonic/Celtic]
' Good, honest, worthy ' (Teutonic) or ' From the yellow house ' (Celtic).
(Stirling)

Sterne [Anglo-Saxon]
' The austere one; an ascetic '.
(Stern, Stearne, Stearn)

Steven See **Stephen**

Stewart [Anglo-Saxon]
' The steward '. Name of the Royal House of Scotland.
(Steward, Stuart, Stew, Stu)

Stillman [Anglo-Saxon]
' Quiet and gentle man '.
(Stilman)

Stinson [Anglo-Saxon]
' Son of stone '.

Stirling See **Sterling**

Stockley [Anglo-Saxon]
' From the cleared meadow '.

Stockton [Anglo-Saxon]
' From the farm in the clearing '.

Stockwell [Anglo-Saxon]
' From the well in the clearing '.

Stoddard [Anglo-Saxon]
' The horse keeper '.

Stoke [Anglo-Saxon]
' A village '.

Storm [Anglo-Saxon]
' The tempest '.

Storr [Scandinavian]
' Great man '.

Stowe [Anglo-Saxon]
' From the place '.

Strahan [Gaelic]
' The poet '.

Stratford [Anglo-Saxon]
' The street crossing the ford '.

Stroud [Anglo-Saxon]
' From the thicket '.

Struthers [Gaelic]
' From the rivulet '.
(Strothers)

Stuart See **Stewart**

Styles [Anglo-Saxon]
' From the dwelling by the stile '.
(Stiles)

Suffield [Anglo-Saxon]
' From the south field '.

Sullivan [Gaelic]
' Man with black eyes '.
(Sullie, Sully)

Sully [Anglo-Saxon]
' From the south meadow '.
Also dim. of Sullivan.

Sumner [Latin]
' One who summons '. The

church official who summoned the congregation to prayer.

Sutcliffe [Anglo-Saxon]
'From the south cliffe'.
(Sutcliff)

Sutherland [Scandinavian]
'From a southern land'.

Sutton [Anglo-Saxon]
'From the south town'.

Swain [Angli-Saxon]
'Herdsman' or 'Knight's attendant'.
(Sweyn, Swayne)

Sweeney [Gaelic]
'Little hero'.

Swinton [Anglo-Saxon]
'From the pig farm'.

Sydney See **Sidney**

Sylvester See **Silas**

Symington [Anglo-Saxon]
'From Simon's farm'.

Girls

Tabitha [Aramaic]
'The gazelle'. One of gentle grace.
(Tabithe, Tabbie, Tabby)

Tacitah [Latin]
'Silence'.
(Tacita)

Tacy [Latin]
'Peace'.

Talitha [Aramaic]
'The maiden'.

Tallulah [American Indian]
'Laughing water'. One who bubbles like a spring.
(Tallula, Tallu, Tally, Tallie)

Tamara [Hebrew]
'Palm tree'.
(Tama, Tammie, Tammy)

Tammy [Hebrew]
'Perfection'. Also dim. of Tamara.

Tamsin See **Thomasina**

Tangerine [Ango-Saxon]
'Girl from Tangiers'.

Tania [Russian]
'The fairy queen'. Also dim. of Titania.
(Tanya)

Tansy [Latin]
'Tenacious'. A woman of determination.

Tara [Gaelic]
'Towering rock'. The home of the ancient kings of Ireland.

Tempest [French]
'Stormy one'.
(Tempesta, Tempeste)

Terentia [Greek]
'Guardian'. Fem. of Terence.
(Terencia, Teri, Terri, Terrie, Terry)

Teresa [Greek]
'The harvester'.
(Theresa, Therese, Terese, Teressa, Teresita, Toireasa, Terri, Terrie, Terry, Tessa, Tessie, Tessy, Tess, Tracie, Tracy, Zita)

Terry See **Terentia/Teresa**

Tertia [Latin]
'Third child'.

Tessa [Greek]
'Fourth child'. Also var, of Teresa.

Thaddea [Greek]
'Courageous being'. A girl of great bravery and endurance.
(Thada, Thadda)

Thalassa [Greek]
'From the sea'.

Thalia [Geek]
'Luxurious blossom'.

Thea [Greek]
'Goddess'. Also dim. of Dorothea, Theadora, Anthea, etc.

Theano [Greek]
'Divine name'.
(Theana)

Thecla [Greek]
'Divine follower'. A disciple of St. Paul.
(Tecla, Thekla)

Theda See **Theodora**

Thelma [Greek]
'The nursling'.

Theodora [Greek]
'Gift of God'. Another version of Dorothy.
(Theda, Theadora, Theadosia, Theodosia, Teodora, Teodore, Dora, Fedora, Fedore, Feodora, Feodore, Feadore, Feadora, Teddie, Theo, Thea and all forms of *Dorothy)*

Theodosia See **Theodora**

Theola [Greek]
'Sent from God'.
(Theo, Lola)

Theone [Greek]
'In the name of God'.
(Theona)

Theophila [Greek]
'Appearance of God'.
(Theaphania, Theafania, Theophanie, Theofanie, Tiffanie, Tiffy)

Theophania [Greek]
'Beloved of God'.
(Theofilia, Theofila, Theophilia)

Theora [Greek]
'Watcher for God'.

Thera [Greek]
' Wild, untamed one '.

Thetis [Greek]
' Positive one '. One who knows her own mind.
(Thetys)

Thirza [Hebrew]
' Pleasantness '.
(Thyrza, Tirza)

Thomasina [Hebrew]
' The twin '. Fem. of Thomas.
(Thomasine, Tomasine, Thomase, Thomasa, Tomase, Tomasa, Tomasina, Tamsin)

Thora [Norse]
' Thunder '. From the God of Thunder—Thor.

Thorberta [Norse]
' Brilliance of Thor '.
(Thorberte, Thorbertha, Thorberte)

Thordis [Norse]
' Spirit of Thor '. The sound of thunder.
(Thordia, Thordie)

Thyra [Greek]
' Shield bearer '.

Tibelda [Teutonic]
' Boldest person '.

Tiberia [Latin]
' From the Tiber '. The river of ancient Rome.

Timothea [Geek]
' Honouring God '.
(Tim, Timmie, Timmy)

Tina See **Christine, Martine,** etc.

Tizane [Hungarian]
' A gypsy '. See also Gitana.

Tita [Latin]
' Honoured title '.

Titania [Greek]
' Giantess '. Also the name of the queen of fairies.
(Tania, Tanya)

Tobey [Hebrew]
' God is good '.
(Toby, Tobe, Tobi)

Tonia See **Antonia**

Topaz [Latin]
' The topaz gem '.

Tourmaline [Srilangarese]
' A carnelian '.
(Tourmalina)

Tracy [Gaelic]
' Battler '. Also der. of Teresa.
(Tracey)

Traviata [Italian]
' The frail one '. Traditionally a courtesan.

Trilby [Italian]
' A singer who trills '.

Trista [Latin]
' Melancholia; sorrow '.

Trixie See **Beatrice**

Trudy [Teutonic]
' Loved one '. Also dim. of Gertrude.
(Trudi, Trudie, Trudey)

Typhena [Latin]
' The delicate one '.
(Triphena, Triphenia, Tryphenia)

Tuesday [Anglo-Saxon]
' Born on Tuesday '.

Tullia [Gaelic]
' Peaceful one '.

Tab [Teutonic]
  ' The drummer '.
  (Tabb, Tabby)

Tadd [Celtic]
  ' Father '. Also dim. for
  Thaddeus and Theodore.
  (Tad)

Taffy [Celtic]
  Welsh form of David.

Taggart [Gaelic]
  ' Son of the prelate '.

Talbot [French]
  ' The looter '. One who lived
  by his spoils and pillages.

Tanner [Anglo-Saxon]
  ' Leather worker '.

Tanton [Anglo-Saxon]
  ' From the quiet river farm '.

Tarleton [Anglo-Saxon]
  ' Thor's farm '.

Tate [Anglo-Saxon]
  ' Cheerful '.
  (Tait, Teyte)

Tavis [Celtic]
  ' Son of David '. Also der.
  (Scottish) of Thomas.
  (Tavish, Tevis)

Taylor [Anglo-Saxon]
  ' The Tailor '.
  (Tailor)

Teague [Celtic]
  ' The poet '.

Tearle [Anglo-Saxon]
  ' Stern, severe one '.

Teddy See **Edward**

Tedmond [Anglo-Saxon]
  ' King's protector '.

Telford [French]
  ' Iron hewer '.
  *(Telfer, Telfor, Telfour,
  Taillefer)*

Templeton [Anglo-Saxon]
  ' Town of the temple '.

Tennyson [Anglo-Saxon]
  ' Son of Dennis '.
  (Tenison, Tennison)

Terence [Latin]
  ' Smooth, polished and
  tender '.
  (Terrene, Torrance, Terry)

Terrill [Teutonic]
  ' Follower of Thor '.
  *(Terrell, Tirrell, Tyrrell,
  Terell, Tirell, Tyrell, Terrel,
  Tirrel, Tyrrel)*

Thaddeus [Hebrew/Greek]
  ' Praise to God ' (Hebrew) or
  ' Courageous and stout
  hearted ' (Greek).
  (Tad, Thad, Taddy)

Thaine [Anglo-Saxon]
  ' Warrior attendant '. A military attendant on a king or
  ruler.
  (Thane, Thayne)

Thatcher [Anglo-Saxon]
  ' A thatcher of roofs '.
  (Thatch)

Thaw [Anglo-Saxon]
  ' Ice breaker '. The perfect
  party guest.

Thayer [Anglo-Saxon]
  ' The nation's army '.

Theobald [Teutonic]
' Bold leader of the people '.
(Tybalt, Tibbald, Thibaud, Thibaut, Tioboid)

Theodore [Greek]
' Gift of God '.
(Feodor, Feodore, Tudor, Dore, Ted, Teddie, Teddy)

Theodoric [Teutonic]
' Ruler of the people '. The elected leader.
(Theodorick, Derek, Derrick, Tedric, Derk, Dirk, Ted, Teddie, Teddy)

Theon [Greek]
' Godly man '.

Theron [Greek]
' The hunter '.

Thomas [Hebrew]
' The twin '. The devoted brother.
(Tomas, Tammany, Tam, Tammy, Thom, Tom, Tommy, Massey)

Thor [Scandinavian]
' God of Thunder '. The ancient Norse God.
(Tor)

Thorald [Scandinavian]
' Thor's ruler '. One who ruled in the name of the thunder-god.
(Torald, Thorold, Terrell, Tyrell)

Thorbert [Scandinavian]
' Brilliance of Thor '.
(Torbert)

Thorburn [Scandinavian]
' Thor's bear '.
(Torburn)

Thorley [Anglo-Saxon]
' From Thor's meadow '.
(Torley)

Thormund [Anglo-Saxon]
' Protected by Thor '.
(Thormond, Thurmond, Tormond, Tormund)

Thorne [Anglo-Saxon]
' From the thorn tree '.

Thorndyke [Anglo-Saxon]
' From the thorny ditch '.

Thornley [Anglo-Saxon]
' From the thorny meadow '.
(Thornly, Thorneley, Thorneley)

Thornton [Anglo-Saxon]
' From the thorny place '.

Thorpe [Anglo-Saxon]
' From the small village '.
(Thorp)

Thurlow [Anglo-Saxon]
' From Thor's hill '.

Thurston [Anglo-Saxon]
' Thor's jewel '.
(Thurstan)

Tierman [Gaelic]
' Lord and master '. The overlord or lord of the manor.
(Tierney)

Tiffany [French]
' The divine appearance of God '.

Tilden [Anglo-Saxon]
'From the fertile valley'.

Tilford [Anglo-Saxon]
'From the good man's farm'.

Timon [Greek]
'Honour, reward, value'.

Timothy [Greek]
'Honouring God'.
(Tim, Timmie, Timmy, Tio-moid)

Tirrell See **Terrell**

Titus [Greek/Latin]
'Of the giants' (Greek) or
'Saved' (Latin).

Tobias [Hebrew]
'God is good'.
(Tobe, Toby, Tioboid, Tobit)

Todd [Latin]
'The fox'.

Toft [Anglo-Saxon]
'A small farm'.

Toland [Anglo-Saxon]
'Owner of taxed land'.

Tomkin [Anglo-Saxon]
'Small Thomas'.
(Tomlin)

Torbert See **Thorbert**

Torley See **Thorley**

Tormey [Gaelic]
'Thunder spirit'.
(Tormy)

Torr [Anglo-Saxon]
'From the tower'.

Torrance [Gaelic]
'From the little hills'. Also
der. of Terence.

Townley [Anglo-Saxon]
'From the town meadow'.
(Townly)

Townsend [Anglo-Saxon]
'From the end of the town'.

Tracy [Latin]
'Bold and courageous'.

Trahern [Celtic]
'Iron strength'. One who
could bend an iron bar in his
bare hands.
(Trehern, Trehearn, Tre-hearne, Trahearn, Trahearne)

Travers [Latin]
'From the crossroads'.
(Travis)

Tredway [Anglo-Saxon]
'Mighty warrior'.

Tremayne [Celtic]
'From the house in the rock'.
(Tremaine)

Trent [Latin]
'The torrent'.

Trevelyan [Celtic]
'From Elian's farm'. An old
Cornish name.

Trevor [Gaelic]
'Prudent, wise and discreet'.
One who can be trusted to
keep secrets.

Trigg [Scandinavian]
'True and faithful'.

Tripp [Anglo-Saxon]
'The traveller'.

Tristan [Celtic]
' The noisy one '.
(Tristin, Tristen)

Tristram [Celtic]
' The sorrowful one '. Do not
confuse with Tristan.

Trowbridge [Anglo-Saxon]
' From the tree bridge '.

Troy [French]
' From the land of the people
with curly hair '.

True [Anglo-Saxon]
' Faithful and loyal '.

Truesdale [Anglo-Saxon]
' The home of the beloved
one '.
(Trusdale)

Truman [Anglo-Saxon]
' A faithful follower '. A loyal
servant.
(Trueman, Trumane)

Trumble [Anglo-Saxon]
' Bold and strong '.

Tucker [Anglo-Saxon]
' Cloth thickener '. A var. of
Fuller.

Tudor See **Theodore**

Tully [Gaelic]
' Obedient to the will of
God '.

Tupper [Anglo-Saxon]
' A sheep raiser '. One who
reared and tended sheep.

Turner [Latin]
' Lathe worker '.

Turpin [Scandinavian]
' Thunder like '. Finnish form
of Thor.

Tuxford [Scandinavian]
' From the ford of the champion spear thrower '.

Twain [Anglo-Saxon]
' Divided in two '. A co-heir.

Twitchell [Anglo-Saxon]
' From a narrow passage-
way '.

Twyford [Anglo-Saxon]
' From the twin river '.

Tybalt See **Theobald**

Tye [Anglo-Saxon]
' From the enclosure '.

Tyler [Anglo-Saxon]
' Maker of tiles or bricks '.
(Tiler, Ty)

Tynam [Gaelic]
' Dark; grey '.

Tyrone [Greek]
' The sovereign '.

Tyson [Teutonic]
' Son of the German '.
(Sonny, Ty)

Girls

Uda [Teutonic]
'Prosperous'. A child of fortune.
(Udella, Udelle)

Ula [Celtic/Teutonic]
'Jewel of the sea' (Celtic);
'The inheritor' (Teutonic)
(Oola)

Ulima [Arabic]
'The learned'. A woman wise in counsel.

Ulrica [Teutonic]
'Ruler of all'.
(Ulrika, Rica)

Ultima [Latin]
'The most distant'.

Ulva [Teutonic]
'The she-wolf'. A symbol of bravery.

Una [Latin]
'One'. The one and only girl.
(Ona, Oona, Oonagh)

Undine [Latin]
'A wave'. The wave of water.

Urania [Greek]
'Heavenly'. The Muse of Astronomy.

Ursula [Latin]
'The she-bear'.
(Ursa, Ursel, Ursie, Ursy, Ursulette, Ursola, Ursule, Ursuline, Orsa, Orsola)

Udell [Anglo-Saxon]
' From the yew tree valley '.

Udolf [Anglo-Saxon]
' Prosperous wolf '.

Ulger [Anglo-Saxon]
' Courageous wolf (spearman) '.

Ulfred [Anglo-Saxon]
' Peace of the wolf '.

Ullock [Anglo-Saxon]
'Sport of the wolf '.

Ulmer [Anglo-Saxon]
' Famous wolf '.
(Ulmar)

Ulric [Teutonic]
' Ruler of all '.
(Alric, Ulrich)

Ulysses [Greek]
' The angry one; the hater '.
(Ulises, Uillioc)

Unwin [Anglo-Saxon]
' The enemy '.

Upton [Anglo-Saxon]
' From the hill farm '.

Upwood [Anglo-Saxon]
' From the hill forest '.

Urban [Latin]
' From the city '. A townsman.

Uriah [Hebrew]
' The Lord is my light; the Lord's light '.
(Urias, Uriel)

Urson See **Orson**

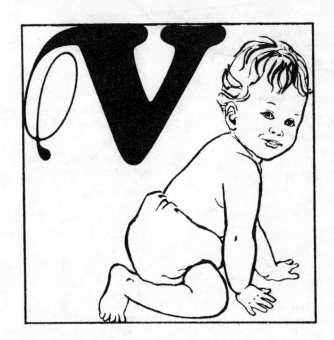

Girls

Vala [Teutonic]
'The chosen one'. Ideal name for the adopted daughter.

Valborga [Teutonic]
'Protecting ruler'.
(Walburga, Walborga, Valburga)

Valda [Teutonic]
'Ruler'.

Valentina [Latin]
'Strong and vigorous'.
(Valentine, Valencia, Valentia, Valeda, Valida, Val, Vallie)

Valerie [French]
'Strong'.
(Valeria, Valery, Valory, Valorie, Valorey, Valora, Val, Vallie)

Valeska [Slavic]
'Glorious ruler'.
(Waleska)

Valonia [Latin]
'From the vale'.
(Valona)

Vanessa [Greek]
'The butterfly'. A name also derived by Jonathan Swift

from 'Ether van Homrigh', one of his correspondents.
(Van, Vanni, Vannie, Vanny, Vanna, Vania, Vanya)

Vanora See Guinevere

Varina [Slavic]
'Stranger'.

Vahsti [Persian]
'Beautiful one'.

Veda [Sanskrit]
'Wisdom and knowledge'.
(Vedis)

Vedette [Italian]
'The sentinel'.
(Vedetta)

Velda [Teutonic]
'Very wise'.
(Valida)

Vega [Arabic]
'The great one'.

Velika [Slavic]
'The falling one'.
(Velica)

Velma See Wilhelmina

Velvet [English]
'Soft as velvet'.

Ventura [Spanish]
'Happiness and good luck'.

Venus [Latin]
'Loveliness; beauty'. The Goddess of Beauty and Love.
(Venita, Vinita, Vinny, Vinnie)

Venetia [Latin]
'Lady of Venice'.

Vera [Latin]
'Truth'. One who is honest and steadfast.
(Vere, Verena, Verene, Verina, Verine, Verla)

Verbena [Latin]
'The sacred bough'.

Verda [Latin]
'Fresh youth'. The verdant qualities of spring.

Verna [Latin]
'Spring like'.
(Vernice, Vernita, Verneta, Verda, Verena, Vernis, Virna, Virina)

Verona [Latin]
'Lady of Verona'. Also dim. of Veronica.

Veronica [Latin]
'True image'. Also var. of Bernice.
(Verona, Vonnie, Vonny, Ronnie, Ronny, and all var. of Bernice)

Vespera [Latin]
'The evening star'.

Vesta [Latin]
'Guardian of the sacred flame'. A Vestal virgin.
'Melodious one'.

Vevay See Vivan

Vevila [Gaelic]
'Melodious one'.

Victoria [Latin]
'The victorious one'.
Attained popularity in Britain following the long reign of Queen Victoria.
(Victorine, Vitoria, Vittoria, Victorie, Vicki, Vicky)

Vida [Hebrew]
' Beloved one'. Fem. of David.

Vidonia [Portuguese]
' Vine branch'.

Vigilia [Latin]
' The alert; vigilant'.

Vignette [French]
' The little vine'.

Villette [French]
' From the village'.

Vina [Spanish]
' From the vineyard'.

Vincentia [Latin]
' The conqueror'. Fem. of Vincent.
(Vincencia, Vicenta)

Vinita See **Venus**

Violet [Latin]
' Modest flower'. Like the shy, retiring violet.
(Viola, Violetta, Violette, Vi, Iolanthe, Yolanda, Yolande, Yolanthe, Violante)

Virgilia [Latin]
' The staff bearer'.

Virginia [Latin]
' The virgin; maidenly and pure'.
(Virginie, Virgi, Virgie, Virgy, Ginger, Ginny, Ginnie, Jinny)

Viridis [Latin]
' The green bough'.

Vita [Latin]
' Life'. One who likes living.
(Veta, Vitia)

Vivian [Latin]
' Alive'. Vivid and vibrant with life.
(Viviana, Vivien, Vivienne, Vivienna, Vivyan, Vyvyan, Viviane, Viviene, Viv, Vivi, Vivia, Vivie)

Volante [Latin]
' The flying one'. One who steps so lightly that she seems to fly.

Voleta [French]
' A floating veil'.
(Voletta)

Vonny See **Veronica**

Vachel [French]
'Little cow'.

Vail [Anglo-Saxon]
'From the valley'.
(Vale, Valle)

Val (Teutonic)
'Mighty power'. Also dim.
for any name beginning with
'Val'.

Valdemar [Teutonic]
'Famous ruler'.
(Valdimar, Valdemar)

Valentine [Latin]
'Healthy, strong and valorous'.
*(Valentin, Valentino, Vailin-
tin, Valente, Valiant)*

Valerian [Latin]
'Strong and powerful' or
'Belonging to Valentine'.

Vallis [French]
'The Welshman'.

Van [Dutch]
'From' or 'Of'. More generally used as a prefix to a surname, but occasionally found
on its own as a forename.

Vance [Anglo-Saxon]
'From the grain barn'.

Varden [Anglo-Saxon]
'From a green hill'.
(Vardon, Verden, Verdon)

Varian [Latin]
'Changeable'.

Vaughan [Celtic]
'The small one'.
(Vaughn, Vawn)

Vere [Latin]
'Faithful and true'. The
loyal one.

Vernon [Latin]
'Growing, flourishing'. As
the trees in spring.
(Verne, Verner, Vern)

Verney [French]
'From the alder grove'.

Verrell [French]
'The honest one'.
(Verrall, Verrill, Verill)

Vick See **Victor**

Victor [Latin]
'The conqueror'.
(Vic, Vick, Victoir)

Vincent See **Victor**

Vinson [Anglo-Saxon]
'Son of Vincent'.

Virgil [Latin]
'Staff bearer' or 'Strong and
flourishing'.
(Vergil, Virge, Virgie, Virgy)

Vito [Latin]
'Alive; vital'.

Vivien [Latin]
'Lively one'.
(Vivian)

Vladimir [Slavic]
'Royally famous'. A re-
nowned monarch.

Vladislav [Slavic]
'Glorious ruler'.

Girls

Walda See **Valda**

Wallis [Anglo-Saxon]
'The Welshwoman; the stranger'.
(Wallace, Wallie, Wally)

Wanda [Teutonic]
'The wanderer'. The restless roamer.
(Wandie, Wandis, Wenda, Wendy, Wendeline)

Wanetta [Anglo-Saxon]
'The pale one'.
(Wanette)

Warda [Teutonic]
'The guardian'.

Welda See **Valda**

Wendy See **Gwendoline, Wanda**

Wilhelmina [Teutonic]
'The protectress'. One who guards resolutely what is her own.
(Wilma, Welma, Velma, Willa, Willie, Willy, Minnie, Minny, Billie, Billy, Helma, Mina)

Wilfreda [Teutonic]
' The peacemaker '. Fem. of Wilfred.
(Wilfrieda, Wilfreida, Freda, Wilf, Freddie)

Willa [Anglo-Saxon]
' Desirable '. Also dim. of Wilhelmina.

Winifred [Teutonic]
' Peaceful friend '. A restful person to have around.
(Winifrida, Winifreida, Winifrieda, Winnie, Winny)

Winola [Teutonic]
' Gracious friend '.

Winona [American Indian]
' First born daughter '.
(Winonah, Wenona, Wenonah)

Wynne [Celtic]
' Fair, white maiden '.
(Win, Wyne)

Wace [Anglo-Saxon]
' A vassal '.

Wade [Anglo-Saxon]
' Mover; wanderer '.

Wadley [Anglo-Saxon]
' From the wanderer's
meadow'.

Wadsworth [Anglo-Saxon]
' From the wanderer's estate '.

Wagner [Teutonic]
' A waggoner '.

Wainwright [Anglo-Saxon]
' Waggon maker '.

Waite [Anglo-Saxon]
' A guard; a watchman '.

Wake [Anglo-Saxon]
' Alert and watchful '.

Wakefield [Anglo-Saxon]
' From the west field'.

Wakeley [Anglo-Saxon]
' From the wet meadow'.

Wakeman [Anglo-Saxon]
' Watchman '.

Walby [Anglo-Saxon]
' From the ancient walls '.

Walcott [Anglo-Saxon]
' Cottage dweller '.

Waldemar See **Valdemar**

Walden [Anglo-Saxon]
' Dweller in the valley in the
woods'.

Waldo [Teutonic]
' The ruler '.

Waldron [Teutonic]
' Strength of the raven '.

Walker [Anglo-Saxon]
' The walker '.

Wallace [Anglo-Saxon]
' The Welshman; the
stranger '.
*(Wallis, Walsh, Welch,
Welsh, Wallache, Wallie,
Wally)*

Walmond [Teutonic]
' Mighty protector '.
(Walmund)

Walter [Teutonic]
' Mighty warrior '.
*(Walther, Walters, Wat,
Wally, Walt)*

Walton [Anglo-Saxon]
' From the forest town '.

Walworth [Anglo-Saxon]
' From the stranger's farm '.

Walwyn [Anglo-Saxon]
' Friendly stranger '.

Warburton [Anglo-Saxon]
' From the castle town '.

Ward [Anglo-Saxon]
' Watchman; guardian '.

Wardell [Anglo-Saxon]
' From the hill watch '.

Warden [Anglo-Saxon]
' The guardian .'

Wardley [Anglo-Saxon]
' From the watchman's
meadow'.

Ware [Anglo-Saxon]
' Prudent one'. A very astute
person.

Warfield [Anglo-Saxon]
' From the field by the weir '.

Warford [Anglo-Saxon]
'From the ford by the weir'.

Waring See **Warren**

Warley [Anglo-Saxon]
'From the meadow by the weir'.

Warmund [Teutonic]
'Loyal protector'.
(Warmond)

Warner [Teutonic]
'Protecting army'.
(Werner, Verner)

Warren [Teutonic]
'The gamekeeper'. One who looked after the game preserves.

Warton [Anglo-Saxon]
'From the farm by the weir'.

Warwick [Anglo-Saxon]
'Strong fortress'.
(Warrick)

Washburn [Anglo-Saxon]
'From the river in spate'.

Washington [Anglo-Saxon]
'From the keen eyed one's farm'.

Watford [Anglo-Saxon]
'From the hurdle by the ford'.

Watkins [Anglo-Saxon]
'Son of Walter'.
(Watson)

Waverley [Anglo-Saxon]
'The meadow by the aspen trees'.
(Waverly)

Wayland [Anglo-Saxon]
'From the pathway near the highway'.

Wayne [Teutonic]
'Waggon maker'.
(Waine, Wain)

Webb [Anglo-Saxon]
'A weaver'.
(Webber, Weber, Webster)

Webley [Anglo-Saxon]
'From the weaver's meadow'.

Weddell [Anglo-Saxon]
'From the wanderer's hill'.

Welborne [Anglo-Saxon]
'From the spring by the brook'.
(Welbourne)

Welby [Anglo-Saxon]
'From the farm by the spring'.

Weldon [Anglo-Saxon]
'From the well on the hill'.

Welford [Anglo-Saxon]
'From the ford by the spring'.

Wellington [Anglo-Saxon]
'From the rich man's farm'.

Wells [Anglo-Saxon]
'From the spring'.

Welsh See **Wallace**

Welton [Anglo-Saxon]
'From the farm by the spring'.

Wenceslaus [Slavic]
'Wreath of glory'.
(Wenceslas)

Wendell [Teutonic]
'The wanderer'.
(Wendel)

Wentworth [Anglo-Saxon]
'Estate belonging to the white haired one'.

Werner See Warner

Wesley [Anglo-Saxon]
'From the west meadow'.
(Wesleigh, Westleigh)

Westbrook [Anglo-Saxon]
'From the west brook'.

Westby [Anglo-Saxon]
'From the homestead in the west'.

Westcott [Anglo-Saxon]
'From the west cottage'.

Weston [Anglo-Saxon]
'From the west farm'.

Wetherell [Anglo-Saxon]
'From the sheep hill'.
(Wetherill, Wetherall)

Wetherley [Anglo-Saxon]
'From the sheep meadow'.
(Wetherly)

Wharton [Anglo-Saxon]
'Farm in the hollow'.

Wheatley [Anglo-Saxon]
'From the wheat meadow'.

Wheeler [Anglo-Saxon]
'The wheel maker'.

Whitcomb [Anglo-Saxon]
'From the white hollow'.
(Whitcombe)

Whistler [Anglo-Saxon]
'The whistler; the piper'.

Whitby [Anglo-Saxon]
'From the white farmstead'.

Whitelaw [Anglo-Saxon]
'From the white hill'.

Whitfield [Anglo-Saxon]
'From the white field'.

Whitford [Anglo-Saxon]
'From the white ford'.

Whitley [Anglo-Saxon]
'From the white meadow'.

Whitlock [Anglo-Saxon]
'White haired one'.

Whitman [Anglo-Saxon]
'White haired man'.

Whitmore [Anglo-Saxon]
'From the white moor'.

Whitney [Anglo-Saxon]
'From the white island'.
(Whitny, Witney, Witny)

Whittaker [Anglo-Saxon]
'One who dwells in the white field'.
(Whitaker)

Wickham [Anglo-Saxon]
'From the enclosed field by the village'.
(Wykeham)

Wickley [Anglo-Saxon]
'From the village meadow'.

Wilbur [Teutonic]
'Resolute and brilliant'. A determined and clever person.

Wiley See William

Wilford [Anglo-Saxon]
'From the willow ford'.

Wilfred [Teutonic]
' Firm peace maker '. Peace, but not at any price.
(Wilfrid, Fred, Freddie, Freddy)

Will See **William**

Willard [Anglo-Saxon]
' Resolute and brave '.

William [Teutonic]
' Determined protector '. The strong guardian.
(Wiley, Wilkie, Wilkes, Wilson, Williamson, Willis, Wilhelm, Willet, Will, Willie, Willy, Bill, Billie, Billy, Uilleam, Uilliam)

Willoughby [Anglo-Saxon]
' From the farmstead by the willows '.

Wilmur [Teutonic]
' Resolute and famous '. One renowned for his firmness.

Wilmot [Teutonic]
' Resolute mind '. One who knows his own mind.

Wilson See **William**
Also ' Son of William ' (Anglo-Saxon).

Wilton [Anglo-Saxon]
' From the farm by the well '.

Winchell [Anglo-Saxon]
' The bend in the road '.

Windsor [Anglo-Saxon]
' The boundary bank '.

Winfield [Anglo-Saxon]
' From a friend's field '.

Winfred [Anglo-Saxon]
' Peaceful friend '.
(Winifred)

Wingate [Anglo-Saxon]
' From the winding lane '.

Winslow [Anglo-Saxon]
' From a friend's hill '.

Winston [Anglo-Saxon]
' From a friend's estate '.

Winter [Anglo-Saxon]
' Born during winter months '.

Winthrop [Teutonic]
' From a friendly village '.

Winton [Anglo-Saxon]
' From a friend's farm '.

Winward [Anglo-Saxon]
' From the friendly forest '.
(Winwald)

Wirth [Teutonic]
' The master '.
(Wirt)

Witter [Teutonic]
' Wise warrior '.
(Witt)

Witton [Teutonic]
' From a wise man's farm '.

Wolcott [Anglo-Saxon]
' From the cottage of the wolf '.
(Wulcott)

Wolfe [Teutonic]
' A wolf '. A man of courage.

Wolfgang [Teutonic]
' The advancing wolf '. A warrior in the vanguard of the army.

174

Wolfram [Teutonic]
'Respected and feared'.

Woodley [Anglo-Saxon]
'From the forest meadow'.
(Woodly)

Woodrow [Anglo-Saxon]
'From the hedge in the wood'.

Woodruff [Anglo-Saxon]
'Forest bailiff'.

Woodward [Anglo-Saxon]
'Forest guardian'.

Woolsey [Anglo-Saxon]
'Victorious wolf'.
(Wolsey, Wolseley)

Worcester [Anglo-Saxon]
'Camp in the forest of the alder trees'.
(Wooster)

Wordsworth [Anglo-Saxon]
'From the farm of the wolf'.

Worrall [Anglo-Saxon]
'From the loyal man's manor'.
(Worrell, Worrill)

Worth [Anglo-Saxon]
'The farmstead'.

Worton [Anglo-Saxon]
'From the vegetable farm'.

Wray [Scandinavian]
'Dweller in the house on the corner'.

Wren [Celtic]
'The chief'.

Wright [Anglo-Saxon]
'Craftsman in woodwork; a carpenter'.

Wyatt See **Guy**

Wyborn [Scandinavian]
'Warrior bear'.
(Wyborne)

Wycliff [Anglo-Saxon]
'From the white cliff'.

Wylie [Anglo-Saxon]
'The enchanter; the beguiler'.

Wyman [Anglo-Saxon]
'The warrior'.

Wymer [Anglo-Saxon]
'Renowned in battle'.

Wyndham [Anglo-Saxon]
'From the village with the winding path'.
(Windham)

Wynn [Celtic]
'The fair one'.

Wythe [Anglo-Saxon]
'From the dwelling by the willow tree'.

Girls

Xanthe [Greek]
  ' Golden blonde '.

Xanthippe [Greek]
  The wife of Socrates

Xaviera [Spanish]
  ' Owner of the home '.

Xena [Greek]
  ' Hospitality '.
  (Xenia, Xene, Zenia)

Xylia [Greek]
  ' From the woods '.
  (Xylona)

Xavier [Spanish/Arabic]
' New house owner ' (Spanish)
or ' Bright ' (Arabic).
(Javier)

Xenos [Greek]
' The stranger '.

Xerxes [Persian]
' The king '.

Xylon [Greek]
' From the forest '.

177

Girls

Yasmine See Jasmine

Yedda [Anglo-Saxon]
'The singer'. One with a
melodious voice.

Yetta [Anglo-Saxon]
'To give, the giver'. Also
dim. of Henrietta.

Ynez See Agnes

Yolanda See Violet

Yvonne [French]
'Archer with the yew bow'.
*(Yvette, Yvetta, Yvona,
Yevetta, Yevette, Ivonne,
Von, Vonnie)*

Yale [Teutonic/Anglo-Saxon]
' The one who pays' (Teutonic)—the vanquished; or
' From the corner of the land '
(Anglo-Saxon).

Yancy [American Indian]
' The Englishman '. Name
given to settlers in New England and subsequently became
Yankee.

Yates [Anglo-Saxon]
' The dweller at the gates '.

Yehudi [Hebrew]
' Praise be the Lord '.

Yeoman [Anglo-Saxon]
' The tenant farmer '.

York [Latin/Anglo-Saxon/
Celtic]
' Boar estate ' (Anglo-Saxon)
' Sacred tree ' (Latin) or
' Yew tree estate ' (Celtic).
(Yorke, Yorick)

Yules [Anglo-Saxon]
' Born at Christmas '.
(Yule)

Yves See Ives

Girls

Zabrina [Anglo-Saxon]
‘ Noble maiden ’.

Zada [Arabic]
‘ Lucky one ’. Fortune’s fav-
ourite.

Zandra See **Alexandra**

Zaneta See **Jane**

Zara [Hebrew]
‘ Brightness of dawn ’. Also
der. of Sarah.

Zea [Latin]
‘ Ripened grain ’.

Zebada [Hebrew]
‘ Gift of the Lord ’.

Zelda See **Grizelda**

Zelia [Greek]
‘ Zealous one ’. One with a
true devotion to duty.
(Zele, Zelie, Zelina)

Zelma See **Anselma**

Zenia/Zenaida See **Zenobia**

Zena [Greek]
‘ The hospitable one ’.

Zenobia [Greek]
 ' Zeus gave life '.
 (Zena, Zenaida, Zenda, Zenna, Zenia, Zenina, Zennie, Zenorbie)

Zera [Hebrew]
 ' Seeds '.

Zerlinda [Hebrew]
 ' Beautiful as the dawn '.

Zerlina [Teutonic]
 ' Serene beauty '.
 (Zerline, Zerla)

Zetta [Anglo-Saxon]
 ' Sixth born '. The sixth letter of the Greek alphabet.
 (Zitao)

Zeva [Greek]
 ' Sword '.

Zilla [Hebrew]
 ' Shadow '.
 (Zillah)

Zinnia [Latin]
 ' The zinnia flower '.
 (Zinia)

Zippora [Hebrew]
 ' Trumpet ' or ' Sparrow '.
 (Zipporah)

Zita See **Zeta, Rosita, Theresa**

Zoë [Greek]
Life

Zona [Latin]
 ' A girdle '. The belt of Orion.
 (Zonie)

Zora [Latin]
 ' The dawn '.
 (Zorina, Zorine, Zorana, Zorah)

Zuleika [Arabic]
 ' Fair '.

Zsa-Zsa See **Susan**

Zacharias [Hebrew]
'The Lord has remembered'.
(Zachariah, Zachary, Zach, Zack)

Zadok [Hebrew]
'The righteous one'.
(Zaloc)

Zane See **John**

Zared [Hebrew]
'The ambush'.

Zebulon [Hebrew]
'The dwelling place'.
(Lonny, Zeb)

Zedekiah [Hebrew]
'The Lord's justice'.

Zeeman [Dutch]
'The sailor'.

Zeke See **Ezekiel**

Zelotes [Greek]
'The zealous one'.

Zelig [Teutonic]
'Blessed one'.

Zenas [Greek]
'Living being'.

Zeus [Greek]
'Father of the gods'.

Zuriel [Hebrew]
'The Lord is my rock and foundation'.

Other titles of interest from Foulsham:

BEFORE BABY ARRIVES
YOUR BABY EQUIPMENT
YOUR BABY'S DEVELOPMENT
BABY TOYS THAT BUILD SKILLS

Notes

Notes

Notes

Notes

Notes

Notes

Notes